DON'T CHANGE THE LIGHT BULBS

CURATED BY RACHEL JONES

A COMPENDIUM OF EXPERTISE FROM THE UK'S MOST SWITCHED-ON EDUCATORS

Crown House Publishing Limited
www.crownhouse.co.uk

First published by

Crown House Publishing Ltd
Crown Buildings, Bancyfelin, Carmarthen, Wales, SA33 5ND, UK
www.crownhouse.co.uk

© Crown House Publishing 2014

Illustrations (in order of appearance) © lily - Fotolia.com, © Comugnero Silvana - Fotolia.com, © Stuart Miles - Fotolia.com, © Heater - Fotolia.com, © puckillustrations - Fotolia.com, © Feng Yu - Fotolia.com, © fotogestoeber - Fotolia.com, © okalinichenko - Fotolia.com, © Pakhnyushchyy - Fotolia.com, © love1990 - Fotolia.com, © Daniel Coulmann - Fotolia.com, © bahrialtay - Fotolia.com, © Kenishirotie - Fotolia.com, © Arsgera - Fotolia.com, © Irochka - Fotolia.com, © daboost - Fotolia.com, © natanaelginting - Fotolia.com, © magann - Fotolia.com, © alphaspirit - Fotolia.com, © simmittorok - Fotolia.com, © winston - Fotolia.com, © nicotombo - Fotolia.com, © Jessmine - Fotolia.com, © gcpics - Fotolia.com, © Tony Baggett - Fotolia.com, © Erica Guilane-Nachez - Fotolia.com, © iQoncept - Fotolia.com, © Alexey Klementiev - Fotolia.com, © pico - Fotolia.com, © Erica Guilane-Nachez - Fotolia.com, © diez-artwork - Fotolia.com, © lightpixel - Fotolia.com, © Independent Thinking Ltd, © Vitaly Korovin - Fotolia.com, © monticellllo - Fotolia.com, © mstanley13 - Fotolia.com, © opeth91 - Fotolia.com, © Les Evans, © ktsdesign - Fotolia.com, © Mirko Raatz - Fotolia.com, © Mirko Raatz - Fotolia.com, © 21051968 - Fotolia.com, © frenta - Fotolia.com, © Erica Guilane-Nachez - Fotolia.com, © treenabeena - Fotolia.com, © Lance Bellers - Fotolia.com, © Rawpixel - Fotolia.com, © Luis Louro - Fotolia.com, © valentinT - Fotolia.com, © alswart - Fotolia.com, © aurora - Fotolia.com, © olly - Fotolia.com, © arsdigital - Fotolia.com, © fullempty - Fotolia.com, © Sergey Nivens - Fotolia.com, © egon1008 - Fotolia.com, © serega1551 - Fotolia.com, © Monkey Business - Fotolia.com, © Marek - Fotolia.com, © brat82 - Fotolia.com, © umberto leporini - Fotolia.com, © Crown House Publishing Ltd, © nuvolanevicata - Fotolia.com, © Crown House Publishing Ltd, © tashatuvango - Fotolia.com, © beermedia.de - Fotolia.com, © Sergey Nivens - Fotolia.com, © lassedesignen - Fotolia.com, © fazon - Fotolia.com, © vkara - Fotolia.com, © Marek - Fotolia.com, © auryndrikson - Fotolia.com

'I Am' poem © 2004 NCTE/IRA. All rights reserved. ReadWriteThink.

First published 2014.

Crown House Publishing has no responsibility for the persistence or accuracy of URLs for external or third-party websites referred to in this publication, and does not guarantee that any content on such websites is, or will remain, accurate or appropriate.

British Library Cataloguing-in-Publication Data
A catalogue entry for this book is available
from the British Library.

Print ISBN 978-178135211-3
Mobi ISBN 978-178135212-0
ePub ISBN 978-178135213-7
ePDF ISBN 978-178135214-4

Printed and bound in the UK by
Gomer Press, Llandysul, Ceredigion

CONTENTS

Welcome to *Don't Change the Light Bulbs* 1
RACHEL JONES @RLJ1981

THIS MUCH I KNOW ABOUT PROFESSIONAL PRACTICE 3
JOHN TOMSETT @JOHNTOMSETT

SECONDARY LEADERSHIP 5
@CHOCOTZAR

STUDENT EMPOWERMENT 7
SARAH FINDLATER @MSFINDLATER

RETHINKING QUESTIONS 9
DAN WILLIAMS @FURTHEREDAGOGY

DELIVERING PROFESSIONAL DEVELOPMENT 13
STEPHEN LOCKYER @MRLOCKYER

SCIENCE 15
DANIEL HARVEY @DANIELHARVEY9

SHARING IDEAS 17
ROSS MORRISON MCGILL @TEACHERTOOLKIT

SOCIAL SCIENCES 21
CHRIS DEAKIN @SOCIOLOGYHEAVEN

ENGLISH 25
GWEN NELSON @GWENELOPE

SPORT AND PE 31
MATHEW PULLEN @MAT6453

WORKING WITH SEN CHILDREN IN A MAINSTREAM SETTING 33
AMY HARVEY @MS_JAMDANGORY

QUESTIONING STRATEGIES 35
ALEX QUIGLEY @HUNTINGENGLISH

ASSESSMENT FOR LEARNING 39
PHIL STOCK @JOEYBAGSTOCK

TECHNOLOGIES TO PROMOTE CREATIVE LEARNING 45
STEVE WHEELER @TIMBUCKTEETH

SOLO TAXONOMY 49
ANDREW DAY @ANDYPHILIPDAY

ART 53
PETE JONES @PEKABELO

USING THE CLOUD IN EDUCATION 57
DAN LEIGHTON PLUS.GOOGLE.COM@DANLEIGHTONGB @DANHLEIGHTON

CREATIVITY 61
AMJAD ALI @ASTSUPPORTAALI

ASSEMBLIES 63
TOM SHERRINGTON @HEADGURUTEACHER

PRIMARY PRACTITIONER 67
STEPH LADBROOKE @LEARNBUZZ

FOR SLT 73
JILL BERRY @JILLBERRY102

LEARNER VOICE PRIMARY 75
FINLEY, YEAR 3 PUPIL

GOVERNANCE 77
JULIA SKINNER @THEHEADSOFFICE

BUILDING POSITIVE RELATIONSHIPS 79
@ITSMOTHERSWORK

LEARNER VOICE SECONDARY 81
YEAR 9 PUPIL, DYLAN @BOOK_WORM39

COMPUTING 83
ALAN O'DONOHOE @TEKNOTEACHER

CREATING INDEPENDENT LEARNERS 87
DAVE ANDRESS @PROFDAVEANDRESS

INSPECTION 89
MARY MYATT @MARYMYATT

PRIMARY LEADERSHIP 93
EMMA PAYNE @EMMA_PAYNEHT

RE 97
ANDY LEWIS @ITEACHRE @TALKINGDONKEYRE

INCLUSION 99
CHRIS CHIVERS @CHRISCHIVERS2

EDU READS 103
CROWD SOURCED BY JON TAIT @TEAMTAIT

LEARNER VOICE POST 16, YEAR 13 PUPIL 105
AMY KENNETT @AMYKENNETT

HALF THE SCARY FUN 107
IAN GILBERT @THATIANGILBERT

TEN PRE-TEACHING THINKING POINTS FOR LITERACY 111
MARTIN ILLINGWORTH @MARTINILLINGWOR

GEOGRAPHY 113
DAVID ROGERS @DAVIDEROGERS

HEAVY METAL LEADERSHIP 117
@H_METAL_LEADER

LAZY TEACHING 121
JIM SMITH @THELAZYTEACHER

BEING A CONNECTED EDUCATOR 123
MARK ANDERSON @ICTEVANGELIST

SURVIVING YEAR 3
(ESPECIALLY AFTER SEVERAL YEARS IN YEAR 6) 125
BEN WALDRAM @MRWALDRAM

CHALLENGE 127
SHAUN ALLISON @SHAUN_ALLISON

HISTORY 129
HARRY FLETCHER-WOOD @HFLETCHERWOOD

BUILDING STRONG RELATIONSHIPS IN YOUR CLASSROOM 133
TIM TAYLOR @IMAGINEINQUIRY

MATHS 137
IESHA SMALL @IESHASMALL

DRAMA 139
HYWEL ROBERTS @HYWEL_ROBERTS

BLOGGING FOR TEACHERS AND STUDENTS 143
RACHEL ORR @RACHELORR

COMPUTING FOR PRIMARY 147
MARTIN BURRETT @ICTMAGIC

BOTTOM-UP LEADERSHIP 153
KEV BARTLE @KEVBARTLE

POST-COMPULSORY LEARNING 157
THOMAS STARKEY @TSTARKEY1212

PEDAGOGY 159
DEBBIE AND MEL @TEACHERTWEAKS

ENJOY TEACHING ART 163
JO BAKER @JOBAKER9

ORGANISING AN EDU-EVENT 167
DAVID FAWCETT @DAVIDFAWCETT27 AND JENN LUDGATE @MISSJLUD

MODERN LANGUAGES 171
JAN BAKER @JANBAKER97

DIFFERENTIATION 173
SUE COWLEY @SUE_COWLEY

TEN THINGS OFSTED WON'T LIKE 175
ANDREW OLD @OLDANDREWUK

PERFORMING ARTS 181
LISA FERNANDEZ ADAMS @LISAFERNANDEZ78

BEHAVIOUR 183
@CAZZYPOT

RESPECT 187
@BERGISTRA

FOR NQTS 189
ROB WARD @PGCENG

COLLABORATIVE WORKING 191
LISA JANE ASHES @LISAJANEASHES

MUSIC IN AND FOR EVERY LEARNING ENVIRONMENT 195
NINA JACKSON @MUSICMIND

TEACHING WITH LOVE 201
DEBRA KIDD @DEBRAKIDD

USING ICT ACROSS THE CURRICULUM 205
RACHEL JONES @RLJ1981

USING RESEARCH IN SCHOOLS 209
CHRIS WAUGH @EDUTRONIC_NET

DESIGN AND TECHNOLOGY 213
DAVID BLOW @DTBLOW AND AMELIA STONE @REVELL57

SHARING RESPONSIBILITY IN SCHOOL 217
MARTYN REAH @MARTYNREAH

BUSINESS AND ENTERPRISE 219
STEPHEN LOGAN @STEPHEN_LOGAN

MEDIA STUDIES 223
SCOTT HAYDEN @BCOTMEDIA

REMEMBER 231
VIC GODDARD @VICGODDARD

Welcome to *Don't Change the Light Bulbs*

A book of top tips written by brilliant and inspiring teachers, educators and leaders from all over the country, many of whom are experts in their field and shining examples of pedagogical excellence. We can all strive to improve outcomes for our learners and to develop ourselves as practitioners. With its focus on pedagogy and nurturing teaching practice, this book is a step towards helping us to do just that.

This book is intended to be cross-curricular and cross-phase, so you will find hints to improve your practice no matter what or whom you teach. There are not specific sections aimed at primary or secondary – this is to encourage you to browse all the ideas without constraint. Traditional ideas are presented alongside SOLO taxonomy. Classroom practice is juxtaposed with leadership hints. Use this opportunity to break down some of the false dichotomies that we, as educators, often have imposed on us.

A massive thank you is owed to everyone who has contributed to this book – their generosity is huge. Please do follow the contributors on Twitter, and share your own practice and ideas with the wider education community. The profits from this book will be given to a charity to help some of the most vulnerable children in society.

Happy learning and teaching!

RACHEL JONES @RLJ1981

1

THIS MUCH I KNOW ABOUT
PROFESSIONAL PRACTICE

JOHN TOMSETT @JOHNTOMSETT

1. Love your students.

2. Know who's in front of you in the classroom, both as a person and as a student.

3. Always act the grown-up when working with children.

4. Don't plan lessons in too much detail – be ready to change course during a lesson.

5. Students can always do more than you expect of them – always have the highest expectations of your students.

6. Work really hard on improving your students' literacy, no matter what your subject.

7. Expect the very best behaviour from students at all times, including good manners.

8. Never take yourself too seriously, but always be aware of the seriousness/importance of your job as a teacher.

9. Have fun!

10. Ultimately, never forget that the best pastoral care for students from the most deprived socio-economic backgrounds is a great set of examination results.

SECONDARY LEADERSHIP

@CHOCOTZAR

1 Communication is key. You may think you have communicated an idea, a policy, a vision, but you may simply have distributed it. Communication needs everyone to absorb the message and engage with it. Making an announcement in a staff meeting also doesn't work. Consider how the institution will function effectively if there isn't true dialogue. If it is important, it needs more than an email. Otherwise dump it.

2 Recruit the right people, even if they may not be right for the precise job you have. If you are looking for a SENCO and a really strong candidate does not have the experience needed – but has the willingness and determination – hire them. After three years, someone brilliant may have more potential than someone who has learned how to manipulate interviews after 20 years of experience.

3 Quality assurance is the answer to school improvement and the way to evidence impact. Ensure you quality assure the quality assurance – every time you ask heads of department to check books or marking, check them at the same time. If you can't squeeze it in among all your other jobs, how will *they* fit it in? Never ask anyone to do anything you can't do yourself.

Indeed, ask middle leaders to put the programme together themselves.

4 All leaders are leaders of teaching and learning. All leaders should continue to teach, and teach with the door open. Keep your books marked and up to date (if you can't maintain the schedule how will anyone else?), share your resources with colleagues, team teach, be humble, but be one of the best. How will anyone take you seriously if you're never in a classroom?

5 Look after one another. Look after the children and their families. Ensure the right people are in place to help everyone who needs it. Look after your staff – listen to them, trust them, hold them to account and treat them to cakes. Invest in your staff and see everyone as a first team player – from the deputy head teacher to the NQT to the part-time teaching assistant. You lead a team, so make sure the ethos is collective care. Consider buying in flu jabs, private health insurance (yes, I love the NHS too but this may get that crucial maths teacher with the back problem back to work quicker). Smile. A lot.

6 Don't do it for Ofsted. Do it for the children. If it benefits the children, supports their best learning and makes them happy and

successful, this will bring results. If you do it in genuine partnership with your staff, this will bring results. Top-down leadership might get you 'good', but only bottom-up leadership can make you 'outstanding'. Do everything right, and for the right reasons, and Ofsted will take care of itself.

7 Some things fade in and out of fashion, some things come and go from the self-assessment form, but these things *always* matter: literacy, numeracy, inclusion, diversity, community, Every Child Matters, gifted and talented, PSHE and the progress of all students, including those in high profile groupings. Do it because it matters.

8 Be visible. Do you really need to go to that meeting? If it's important, send someone else. Walk the corridors and let the children know you're present and interested. Go into classrooms, join in the learning, talk to people, ask them for their thoughts. Attend school productions, parents' evenings. Do a duty every day – lunch queue, playtime, gate duty. The kids need to know who you are.

9 Don't change the light bulbs. You may want to do your best for your colleagues but your job is not to change the light bulbs, clear up sick, vacuum the carpet or place orders. Delegate. Hold others to account. If they're meant to have changed the light bulbs, but haven't, that's a strong conversation instead.

> ... your job is not to change the light bulbs, clear up sick, vacuum the carpet or place orders.
>
> Delegate.

10 Enjoy it. If you're not enjoying it, why are you doing it? You can't lead a school just for the cash and the holidays; you wouldn't expect it from a teacher you employed. Smile, laugh, have a sense of humour, share jokes with the kids, join in a game of football. Find things that are fun and enjoyable to schedule into the school year. And never get that sinking dread feeling in the pit of your stomach on a Sunday evening.

STUDENT EMPOWERMENT

SARAH FINDLATER @MSFINDLATER

Empower
/em-pow-er/
def: Give someone the authority or power to do something. Most often used in a work or legal environme[nt]

I VALUE WHAT THEY BRING TO THE TABLE

Students are such a rich and vibrant resource in our classrooms that we would be foolish not to tap into them. I have found that getting to know your students and using that knowledge to help shape your lessons is hugely empowering for young people.

II STUDENT VOICE

Giving students a voice will enable them to feel valued, enabling you, your team and the school as a whole to make changes to better everyone's experience in school. Involving them in the consultation process when changes are being made or in forming new school policies ensures that the school and the students are working in unison and everyone involved has a vested interest in being better.

III PUT YOURSELF INTO THE MIX

Overtly showing the learning process in class is a brilliant way to build student confidence. I find that if I model the process when teaching a topic, and create alongside them, they are instantly more confident in their work and will take more risks. There is a feeling of 'we are all in this together'.

IV CHOICE

Giving students options in class is a great way to strengthen student buy-in. For example, simply giving them a choice of task, target, outcome or learning objective can improve participation and interest.

V SELF-ASSESSMENT

Training students to peer and self-assess enables them to take charge of their own progress. Giving students access to the mark scheme and helping them to break it down is essential to empowering them in their work. Sharing success criteria can take the fear out of tasks. We must remember not to make this the main focus of tasks, though, as it can suck the joy out of the classroom. Inspire with the task first and share the success criteria second.

VI   REFLECTION

Ensure ample time is given to student reflection. Students need to be trained in how to reflect effectively – modelling and practice is key to this success. I have found that reflection is most powerful when it is in response to teacher feedback and includes clear and specific student-decided steps for improvement. Students need to put these steps into action soon after committing to them for the full impact to be realised. Do it well, and do it regularly, and students will really move on in their learning and thinking processes.

VII   CELEBRATE SUCCESS

When students get it right celebration is in order. We are so busy as teachers that these moments of wonder can too often pass by unrecognised. We need to refocus on celebrating success to ensure that our students keep on trying to get it right and move themselves on. Celebration may come in many forms and what one student appreciates will be different to another. However we do it, though, it has to be done.

VIII   ENCOURAGE FAILURE

Better to try and fail than never to have tried at all. I actively encourage failure in my classroom as I feel it is the quickest way for students to learn. When it works well students will feel brave enough to go out on a limb and take risks. If you can get to a point with a class where this is commonplace, then it is wonderful place to be.

IX   STUDENT ACCOUNTABILITY

We are empowering the students in our classrooms to take ownership of their actions. If they do something wrong they need to own it. If they are rude to someone they need to own it. If they are not putting full effort into their work they need to own it. If they are not happy with their results they need to own it. With great power comes great responsibility.

X   CHALLENGE AND DEBATE ISSUES TOGETHER

A healthy debate in class is always a great activity. It helps you get to know your students and it can open them up to speak more freely. Debate and discussion is also essential if a student says or does something that is inappropriate in class. This needs to be handled sensitively so as not to offend the perpetrator or those who may feel aggrieved by the comment or action. I try never to leave an issue unrecognised with a class, as it can turn the tide towards negativity and shut down student contributions.

> **Encourage failure.**
> I actively encourage failure in my classroom as I feel it is the quickest way for students to learn.

RETHINKING QUESTIONS

DAN WILLIAMS @FURTHEREDAGOGY

Questioning is one of the greatest tools for a teacher to have in their arsenal. Sound questioning can be the difference between an effective and an ineffective session. I see the purpose of questioning as three-fold: to check understanding, to develop under-

10 Plan for a range of questions to be asked in your session so that all learners are provided with an opportunity to answer. This will include closed, short answer questions, such as 'What is ... ?' or 'Where can ... ?' These questions give the teacher a basic grasp of learner understanding while also allowing for less confident learners to involve themselves. Also, the more learners answer this type of question, the more their confidence and communication skills develop. You should also plan for more open, deeper questions in each session to allow for stretch and challenge, such as 'How might ... ?' or 'Why will ... ?' This type of question provides learners with the opportunity to demonstrate deeper understanding.

9 Pose and pause when asking questions.[1] Once a teacher poses a question, quite often the quickest and most confident learner is the one who gets to answer. This leaves the teacher with very little information as to the understanding of the remainder of the group. By preparing learners prior to the question, by telling them that they will be provided with 'think time', you are allowing those who require a little longer to formulate an answer to become involved. Do not be afraid

to let the classroom go quiet to do this.

8 Pounce on selected learners. Following on from pose and pause, and in order to restrict the quicker and most confident learners from dominating with answers, you can purposely select individuals to answer the question. You may also link this to tip number 10, by selecting individuals based on the difficulty of the question.

7 Pass, or bounce, the question around the classroom. Rather than telling the learner that their answer is correct straight away, try thanking them for their response and selecting another learner to answer the question. By thanking the learner and not giving away the answer immediately, other learners are more willing to offer their thoughts if their response is completely different to the one given. Following a response, you may also ask who agrees or disagrees with it by a show of hands. This allows the teacher to visualise who understands. To ensure that it is not just a case of conformity, the teacher can then select learners to explain why they agree or disagree.

Here is an example of points 9 to 7 in practice:

Pose: Why might we cook chicken on the grill?

Pause: ... (10 seconds)

Pounce: Daniel?

Pass: Thank you. Navneet, can you expand on Daniel's answer?

6 The 'Why?' sequence. When a question is posed to a learner or group, you can stimulate deeper

---

[1] The pose, pause, pounce, bounce technique is described in C. Harrison and S. Howard, *Inside the Primary Black Box: Assessment for Learning in Primary and Early Years Classrooms* (London: GL Assessment, 2009), p. 15.

thought through asking why – over and over. The more you do this, the deeper and wider the thinking. This requires the teacher to be very adaptable and to think on their feet.

The process can be linked to the pose, pause, pounce, pass approach in the following way:

Question: What is citizenship?

Answer: Citizens are members of a state or nation, and citizenship is the process of being a member of such an entity. It is how we make society work, together.

Question: Why is it important?

Answer: It is important because society belongs to all of us and what we put into it creates what we get out of it.

Question: But why bother?

Answer: We want everyone to feel they belong. And we want everyone to feel they can drive change within society.

Question: Why is it important for society to change?

And so on …

5 Question tokens. To ensure that each learner is questioned and asks questions during a session the teacher could provide them with question tokens. The aim is for the learners to lose all of their tokens – for example, they need to ask questions to lose green tokens and answer questions to lose red tokens. This is a great way to ensure differentiation and that everyone is engaged in the session. To further differentiate, learners could be provided with different numbers of tokens depending on their ability.

4 Peer questioning. Peer questions can be organised in many ways. One example is to split the class into small teams. The teams then create questions on a particular topic and ask the other teams their questions. They must know the answer to the questions themselves though. Learners can also lose question tokens to one another by asking and answering questions during paired/group activities. In addition, the teacher may create a class rule whereby any learner who has a question about the topic must ask two or three of their peers prior to asking the teacher for the answer.[2]

3 Reverse questions. Quite simply, the teacher provides learners with the answer to a question and their job is to come up with suitable questions for the answer. The questions they provide can then be assessed for suitability via discussion.

2 Matching pairs Q&A. This is a great starter activity which can engage learners through questions. The teacher provides half of the group with questions related to a topic and the other half with the answers. The learners then need to pair themselves up accordingly. To make the activity more difficult, a few 'red herring' questions and/or answers can be provided. The task offers a perfect opportunity for discussion and further Q&As.

1 Anonymous answers. Some learners feel uncomfortable answering questions out loud, so with this activity the teacher poses a question to learners and allows them to 'post' their answers in a box at the front of the classroom. The teacher can gauge the understanding of the class through a quick look at the responses. A more innovative way of using this activity is through text polls using a website such as www.polleverywhere.com. This site performs a basic analysis of results and displays answers graphically or as a word cloud.

---

2 The 3B4ME idea originally came from a training session with Geoff Petty. It is also covered in G.Petty, *Teaching Today: A Practical Guide*, 4th edn (Cheltenham: Nelson Thornes, 2004).

DELIVERING PROFESSIONAL

1. In *The Jelly Effect* by Andy Bounds,[1] he likens good talks using PowerPoints with news sketches from *The Two Ronnies*. If you say it, don't make your slides say it too – they should complement and not repeat each other.

2. Be really organised. Rehearse as much as you can.

3. Don't read out text from a screen and have as few words on slides as possible.

4. Read everything by Carmine Gallo and Nancy Duarte, especially *Resonate*.[2]

5. Break things down into ten-minute chunks. I do this as a matter of course as I have such a low boredom threshold.

6. See a need, fill a need. Personalise everything as much as possible. The best CPD should have an immediate impact in the next lesson. Is that doable?

---

1 A. Bounds, *The Jelly Effect: How to Make Your Communication Stick* (Chichester: Capstone, 2007).
2 N. Duarte, *Resonate: Present Visual Stories That Transform Audiences* (Hoboken, NJ: John Wiley & Sons, 2010).

7. None of us are the expert, but there is an awful lot of expertise out there. Ask for help - you'll be amazed with what you get back.

8. My friend Alexis Conway (@wherenext5) uses the term PPD (Paired Professional Development), which I think is brilliant. Helping each other out shares the workload and helps guide others.

9. Visibly demonstrate active CPD as much as you can - on wall displays, in the staffroom, in staff meetings. We are all at school to strive to improve. Show the pupils you are learning too.

10. Keep a CPD diary if you can. The site www.ohlife.com is brilliant for this as it helps you to gauge improvement and offers a fantastic perspective too.

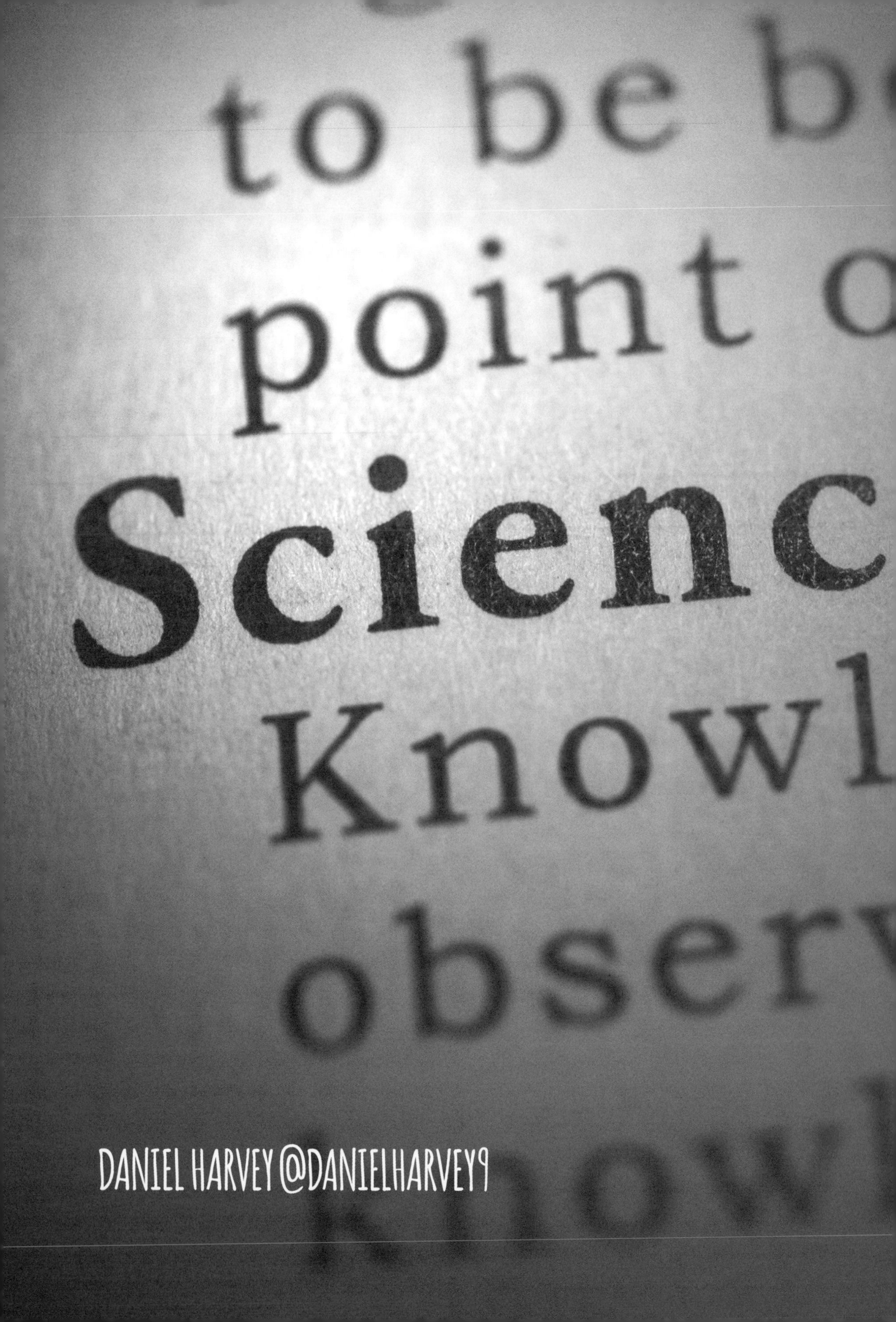
to be b
point o
Scienc
Knowl
observ

DANIEL HARVEY @DANIELHARVEY9

1 Always carry out experiments and demos beforehand to make sure you can do it safely and understand how to explain it to students. Read the safety guidance and double check with science technicians (see also tip number 9).

2 A good demo can be more purposeful and helpful learning than students just carrying out the experiment. The teacher can then draw attention to the key aspects of the demo. When combined with a flexi-cam or visualiser, the teacher can zoom in to make sure the aspects they want students to learn are clearly visible. The teacher can take photos of the demo using the visualiser or camera which can then become writing or task prompts for the students.

3 Science is an umbrella title for the three main disciplines (i.e. biology, chemistry, physics). More often than not, new entrants will have gaps in their understanding of key concepts from the other disciplines. Work to understand these ideas and how to develop students' learning in them. At some point you will need to teach these ideas.

4 Join the Association for Science Education (www.ase.org.uk) and other science teacher organisations, such as:

- Institute of Physics
  www.iop.org

- Royal Society of Chemistry
  www.rsc.org/education

- Society of Biology
  www.societyofbiology.org

All these organisations offer valuable and brilliant CPD which will enhance your understanding of how best to teach scientific ideas and, in turn, the quality of your students' learning.

5 Teach and develop students' knowledge and use of key terms from Years 7 to 13. Scientific literacy is key to exam success and so needs to be explicitly taught, supported and fed back in all year groups. Look at departmental strategies for this and consult others on the best ways to get students to write in depth and to the necessary length.

6 Some mathematical knowledge is essential for a number of science concepts. Forces, motion, chemical moles, mass calculations and estimations are just some examples where certain maths applications are needed to solve problems or find answers. This needs just as much thought and care as literacy, but *don't* comment on your own maths capabilities. Empower students to see that the maths methodology is generally straightforward. You might want to consider a maths mat approach as well.

7 Science is both a discipline and a process. The process needs to be understood by students as much as the content – currently 25% of GCSE and 20% of A level is awarded on applying scientific processes. This means you will have to incorporate practical learning into your lessons. The students should be clear about the concept they are studying and also what process they are learning to apply

successfully. Don't leave it to chance or someone else – develop this process learning yourself. Look at the controlled assessment for GCSE and A level and shape your lessons accordingly, even for Year 7.

8 Talk to your colleagues at work and to contacts elsewhere (e.g. #asechat on Monday nights) to develop your pedagogy in science. These teachers will understand the background and context of your questions and can give grounded, relevant answers. You can also showcase any work you are proud of, or are perhaps developing, and get decent, valid feedback to improve it further. Professional collaboration is a main driver towards enhanced performance so get involved.

> Don't ever forget that science lessons can wow students in ways most other subjects can't.

9 Work with your science department technicians. Describe your thinking and listen to their advice. As a result, your experiments will work better and more often, and you will also find that they suggest other ways of showing the desired effect. In addition, they will be able to point you to current guidance on many experiments.

10 Don't ever forget that science lessons can wow students in ways most other subjects can't. Exploding hydrogen balloons, peroxide snakes, heart dissections, flame tests and bottle rockets can all capture their interest in ways other subjects can only dream about. Use this to your own and your students' advantage! Regularly!

SHARING IDEAS

ROSS MORRISON MCGILL @TEACHERTOOLKIT

I would not be the teacher I am today without having had to evolve my own practice over the past 20 years to meet the needs of my students.

1 Do not sit still. Do all you can to observe colleagues – invite them into your lessons and visit other schools. Read – online or in print. Follow people on blogs or on Twitter and keep up to speed with dialogue across the country. Do whatever is needed to shape your own practice.

2 Get on Twitter. You will receive instant feedback and resources in a millisecond. There is no better way to do it! The benefits of doing this are: (a) you can do this 24/7 and (b) you can get feedback beyond your own institution.

3 Attend TeachMeets. This is the modern way to develop your professional practice in and out of school. If you are brave enough,

present to the audience too. It may be scary, but you will thank yourself for it later and be hooked in no time.

4 What? Why? How? Plan to teach your students to become smarter assessors (#SmartAss). To improve students' understanding of their own work, I embed this simple questioning strategy in all that they do. In all manner of feedback, my students would, for example, spend three minutes reporting back on:

- ■ 'What have I done?' or 'What is on this page?'

- ■ 'Why have I done this?'

- ■ 'How did I do this?' or 'How did I get here?'

17

The smartest way to do this is to get your students to record these responses in a self-analysis speech-bubble, which can often be a doodle on the page. This information is then used to centre discussions, decode or consolidate the learning and inform feedback. Read more here: http://teachertoolkit. me/2013/12/13/i-want-to-be-a-smartass-by-teachertoolkit/.

5 Lesson planning. For me it's all about 'stickability'. What do you want students to bring back to their next lesson with you? This should be the fundamental learning gain in your own lesson planning. It's all I focus on and it significantly reduces planning time. Read more here: http://teachertoolkit. me/2013/06/24/so-what-is-stickability-by-teachertoolkit-head_stmarys/.

6 Google documents. This is my number one teaching resource for the classroom. It can be used to set homework and allow students to access secure documents online. This book used Google Docs as an initial platform to gather chapter ideas. I also use this software with my colleagues in school and further afield online and is the key piece of software that allows @SLTchat to be so successful every Sunday at 8 p.m. I can't share anything without it!

> Speak in front of your peers. Not everyone can and not everybody wants to, but it is the most daunting and yet fulfilling thing you can do in your own place of work.

7 Mindset. Be open and reflective – not everybody is! If you are the type of person who fears critique in your own school, try sharing your teaching ideas anonymously online. There are many others who do this comfortably and very well. Alternatively, share your thoughts in your own blog in order to gain feedback.

8 Speak in front of your peers. Not everyone can and not everybody wants to, but it is the most daunting and yet fulfilling thing you can do in your own place of work. You won't believe the amount of confidence that it will bring you. We do this every day in the classroom, so it should be even easier with a room full of adults who are going to behave!

I have blogged about CPD peer-to-peer at: http://teachertoolkit. me/2014/05/09/peer-to-peer-fear-or-hear-by-teachertoolkit/. Fear or hear – which are you?

If you are stuck on where to start, take a look at @Actionjackson and @DavidMcQueen as well as YouTube videos for tips and advice on public speaking.

9 My penultimate idea stems from the philosophy of Jim Smith (@thelazyteacher): 'you teach less and your students learn more'. How? Well, read his book for full details. There is a huge range of ideas, but the one that sticks with me is

encouraging students to reflect on, feedback and redraft work more often. If your students enjoy redrafting work and can see the benefits, then you will too! Your workload will greatly reduce after the initial change in expectations; students will make more progress over time, and when redrafting is routine you can embed the FAIL (First Attempt In Learning) ethos.

10 Finally, start your own professional blog for reflection, feedback and sharing content. It has transformed my practice as a classroom teacher and school leader, and that can only be a valuable commodity for school improvement. I started out with my very first blog post and just one reader; now, readers of my blog exceed 100,000 every month. And there are unimaginable rewards: opportunities range from visiting new schools, CPD, knocking on the door to Ofsted's headquarters and attending events at the House of Commons. Sharing my views online has led to award ceremonies, writing newspaper articles and being asked to appear at conferences. I was even approached to write my first book and my blog is now ranked as one of the most influential in the UK. All very flattering!

Do not delay. Start today …

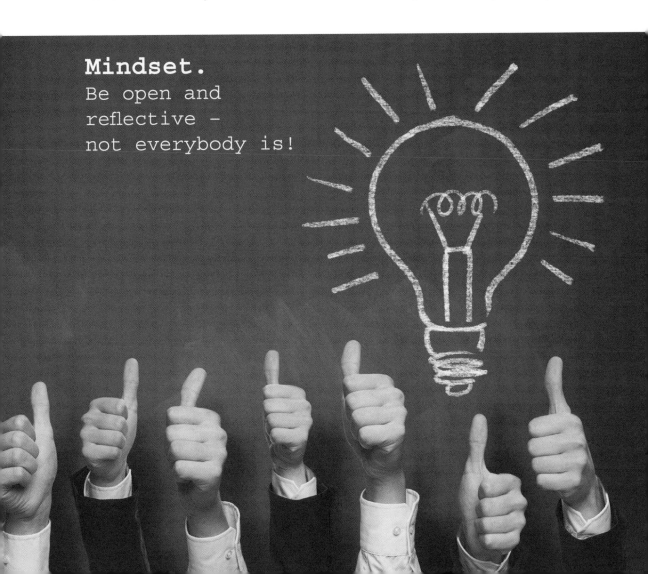

Mindset.
Be open and
reflective –
not everybody is!

SOCIAL SCIENCES

1 FIND A HOOK

The great thing about a subject like sociology is that your subject matter (the issues and concepts) are all around us, all the time. A simple way to engage students is to relate what you are studying to their actual lives. This, in turn, develops the element of relevancy and purpose to the learning taking place, but also it promotes what C. Wright Mills termed a 'sociological imagination' and a critical outlook. In lessons, this may well take the form of an anecdote, a TV storyline or a news story. More effective, though, is finding an activity that delves beneath a concept and its meaning – usually without a sociological reference. For example, take 'alienation', not the easiest beastie to communicate, but establish a reflective exercise around the idea of powerlessness and you're on to a winner. For me, it's sharing experiences of part-time jobs (usually shelf-stacking)

using flip paper and a gingerbread figure to explore experiences, feelings, thoughts and so on.

2 CREATIVE SERENDIPITY

In his landmark text, *The Sociological Imagination*, C. Wright Mills emphasised the value of serendipity in social science.[1] By this he meant the powerful process of making connections between seemingly unconnected phenomena. This is a useful creative process which is central to sociological enquiry and demands that our students think outside of the box. The key thing to keep in mind here is linkage, although the actual link will not be the outcome of this exercise – it is the serendipitous

1 C. Wright Mills, *The Sociological Imagination* (Oxford: Oxford University Press, 1959).

process that matters. Wherever you can, put your students into that 'thinking zone' – you know, that place where there is a degree of tension, stepping beyond the known into somewhere where their imaginations (cognitive engagement) and emotional engagement meet. As the Dodo said in *Alice's Adventures in Wonderland*, 'the best way to explain it is to do it', so let me illustrate with an example. You can do this 'intra-topic' or 'inter-topic' – the latter of these is a bit like what some call 'synopticity'. There are relative merits to both.

At the end of a topic, provide students with a set of numbered key concepts (e.g. (1) dependency culture, (2) same-sex households, (3) domestic labour, (4) social construction of childhood, (5) domestic violence). This list can be based on a glossary from a modern textbook and can be as long as about 100 concepts or more. Use a number generator or select two random numbers from your list and then ask a pair of students to make a link between them (e.g. dependency culture and domestic violence may result in a link like, 'There may be greater levels between those on welfare because of the threats to masculinity experienced by unemployed men who then vent their frustrations on their partners to boost their sense of self-worth'). The link may be tentative and may not be found in a textbook, but the journey from A to B is what counts – synaptic activity abounds. You can, of course, add an image on screen for them to link concepts to, or even ask them to link three or four concepts, which can be fun (my record under challenge was seven!). You can also adapt this and give them a question, some images, concepts and so on, and ask them to make links and 'anchor' their thinking in the given question. Active minds are, of course, what engagement is all about – and sociology is all about active (and critical) thinking.

21

3 MAKING COMPARISONS

Where possible encourage students to compare phenomena. By this I mean encourage students to compare different theories about an issue. This could be described as an A02 skill of 'application' but, in essence, students are simply comparing different theoretical perspectives to a debate/question. The challenge for the teacher is the selection of the themes that you want to apply the theories to.

The value of this approach cannot be understated. We are aiming to develop critical thinkers who can take 'free floating concepts' and use these in various contexts. Too often, the didactic teaching approach, which encourages passivity, leads to an insecurity on the part of learners – hence, they regurgitate these virtually verbatim without understanding the meaning of what they are presenting. We see this too often when we read back a paragraph that is bulging at the seams with sociologists and terms, but the relevancy to the question is very unclear.

Where possible take students off site. … it's worth it.

So, we need to have students focusing on themes and issues more than studies and thinkers. The easiest way to develop this is to allocate a perspective to a different group of students – for example, Functionalism, Marxism, New Right, Feminism, Labelling, Post-Modernism. Then pass around sheets of flipchart paper with different issues for them to focus on, such as, 'Working class educational attainment', 'How to reduce inequality in education', 'Why is the nuclear family the most desirable?' and so on. Students then focus on one issue at a time and each group writes down in a different coloured pen what their perspective would say about this. The groups then pass on the flipchart paper and add their views to the newly arrived sheets. The key is to be selective. They should also add any evaluation points next to the ideas from the other perspectives as they receive them. Students should also be encouraged to insist on clarification of each other's additions and remove anything which is irrelevant (in a positive way, of course). Following the carousel process, each chart should be mounted on the board and used as the basis for a whole-class discussion, with each perspective making their case. An excellent dialogistic (oral literacy) strategy!

4 GET OUT AND ABOUT

Where possible take students off site. I know it's a right pain filling out paperwork in triplicate – all that risk assessment stuff – but it's worth it. The subject matter of sociology is all around us, so exploit it. This may take the form of a location visit, such as the local courtrooms or a community/youth centre on a local housing estate. The latter provides better opportunities for discussion with people about the day-to-day activities that take place. An 'urban trek' is also a good strategy, where you prepare in advance a range of tasks and questions for students to follow (e.g. probing questions about local housing/pricing in estate agent windows). Another useful approach is to use 'methods in context' where students conduct interviews/ questionnaires/observations in the local town.

5 VISITING SPEAKERS

Like arranging visits to locations, it is also invaluable to invite visitors into school. These will depend on the topic being studied, but there is a wealth of useful resources out there. Prior to a visit, help the guest to focus by setting the scene and providing them with a context (e.g. key questions). At the same time, prepare the students and give them time to work out what questions they will ask. (This may need you to go beyond the immediate topic to get the best out of the session – for example, asking a police officer if they think that schools could do more to promote discipline.)

6 METHODS APPLIED

From day one get students thinking methodologically. Initially, this may be designing surveys to identify trends or gauge opinions on exciting topics, like, 'What should be done about crime?', or more populist questions surrounding topics like social networking, drug use and so on. Use these to introduce different research skills throughout a course (e.g. leading questions, biased interpretation, sampling issues). Set up a lesson with a pack of data or artefacts and encourage students to investigate a topic and ask questions – curiosity is all.

> **encourage students to avoid falling into the Wikipedia cut-and-paste trap!**

This is what was so wonderful about Pete Langley's *Discovering Sociology* – it included a set of photos/data and text that encouraged enquiry on key questions.[2] When it comes to units with a 'methods in context' focus, produce booklets with descriptions of a specific method, examples of use and key advantages/disadvantages, followed by a context in which to apply the given method (e.g. participant observation and pupil subcultures (AQA, Unit 2)). It is useful to develop a set of Socratic trigger questions for students to help focus their thinking (e.g. Is sampling straightforward here? Does this method helps us explore meanings/interactions?).

2 P. Langley (ed.), *Discovering Sociology* (Harlow: Causeway Press, 1998).

7 UPDATES

Society doesn't stand still. Students should be encouraged to keep an eye on current affairs and how the topics they are studying evolve around them. Examiners love this sort of awareness as it shows that students are able to move beyond the textbook and 'apply' material to given debates. In my day (ahem!), this was more a case of watching the news or reading a paper. It is much easier for students today, as they have everything from news websites to YouTube to help them stay up to date. Search filters make it a straight-forward process but, as ever, encourage students to avoid falling into the Wikipedia cut-and-paste trap! Try to push them towards more specific and interesting sites (e.g. *The Guardian* and *TES* for education issues).

8 REGULAR ASSESSMENT

Sociology and its content are new to many students, and for some it can be quite daunting. It is important that we therefore build in benchmarks (not just for us to have a measure of progress, but more so for students to see where they are) throughout the year. Key-point testing on a weekly or fortnightly basis can be very useful. These are simple tests of definitions and key ideas. There should be no more than 10 questions and it should take up only a small part of the start of a lesson. Don't worry about the marking workload – have the students swap test papers and mark as you go through the answers and explore responses with them. Don't be afraid to experiment with these: perhaps post the questions online in advance or let students write the questions – sometimes these can be better than what the teacher generates! Assessment can also take the form of 'practising skills'. This may take the form of practising the PEEL (Point, Evidence, Evaluation, Link) paragraph, introductions or evaluation skills. Set up timed answers for students – with a very clear focus established beforehand. Peer assessment should follow with students applying your own rubric that 'tests the skill' being developed.

9 CONCEPTUAL AWARENESS

Find as many opportunities to bed down and develop a deeper understanding of key concepts. Most textbooks have a glossary of terms in the appendices and these should be used to good effect. At the start of each topic, it is a useful strategy to provide students with a glossary comprising the main terms that they will cover, with simple definitions (these can be listed alphabetically, although I prefer to break them up into a chronological order that follows the scheme of work – which helps for setting key-point tests). Devise activities for encouraging students to think about concepts and their meanings. Mix-and-match card sorts are good here. I also suggest having a concept wall visible in your classroom which you can refer to at different points (I add images here to support concept recall – see an example for religion at http://www.youtube.com/watch?v=BqxxGMaubT0).

10 ACTIVE ENGAGEMENT

This doesn't really need to be stated, but it so vital that it must be. Students will thrive within sociology if they are cognitively and emotionally engaged within lessons. As a trainee teacher, I remember a college student turning to me in an observed lesson and uttering the soul-destroying phrase, 'I'm too bored to learn!', and this was long before distractions like the internet had kicked in. There was, however, some truth in where he was at, because the lesson was very teacher-led, with exposition/note taking and then exercises from a textbook. Sociology will die a death if we don't mix it up a bit – and we have the best subject material to have some fun with. My advice is always look for the opportunity to bring it alive with an activity involving pairs or small groups.

Now, there may be times when we have to plough through content for a lesson or so in order to give students enough material to play with. That said, my rule of thumb is, if you've had a content-heavy session or two, then set aside a good hour to bring it to life. Very simply, set them up, step away and let them run with it. In a good active session you will be more of a guide or facilitator who visits groups with differentiated support and motivation throughout. Students love activities where they can take the lead and have space to create something of their own. Ensure that each activity has a 'skills focus' and you won't go wrong. For example, to introduce basic Marxist concepts, set up a role play/simulation where students are divided into workforce and company bosses to highlight the nature of production, profit, labour power and alienation (there is an example of this activity at #52Inspirations). For those who are uncomfortable with role play, active learning may be more a case of mix-and-match cards, diamond nine ranking, model-making and so on. All these have one thing in common: they encourage thinking and develop 'meaningfulness' in learning, which is what all good learning should aspire to achieve.

> … my rule of thumb is, if you've had a content-heavy session or two, then set aside a good hour to bring it to life.

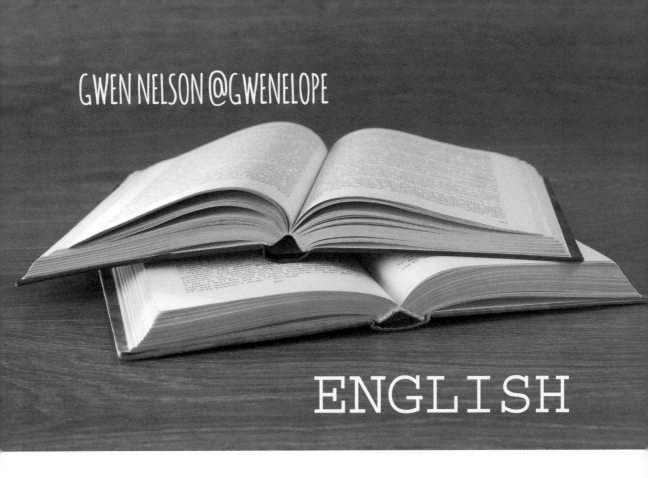

GWEN NELSON @GWENELOPE

ENGLISH

1 'Your first duty, as an English teacher, is to make the pupils love your subject.' This was said to me by an inspirational AST in my NQT year. I have never forgotten it, for good reason. When all around is madness – and, of course, it is for many of us at the moment – remember this while you plan schemes of work and lessons and when you set foot in your classroom.

2 'Literacy is making the implicit explicit to your pupils.' A remark by Geoff Barton at Wellington Educational Festival. This need not merely apply to whole-school literacy but to all aspects of your teaching, specifically when it comes to writing. Write on the board, show pupils your errors, discuss them with pupils, do your thinking aloud. In this way, you model the thought processes concerned with reading and writing for your pupils, and make it clear that making mistakes is a normal part of the writing process.

3 Use images as a way into a text – the more alien the text to the pupils, the more useful images are. For example, I showed an image of the Garden of Eden to a low ability Year 10 class prior to reading *Of Mice and Men*. We discussed what we knew about the Garden of Eden and what the 'moral' of the narrative was – the serpent. Then, after reading the opening chapter, we drew comparisons between the biblical imagery and Steinbeck's description of the pond that George and Lennie arrive at in Chapter 1. The image prompted some higher level thinking from these pupils who generally lack confidence in expressing an opinion in English

25

lessons. The image provided them with a means to express their ideas.

4 Novels are a joy and always one of my favourite things to teach. I have often stuck too rigidly to reading the text as a whole class, but have fared better when more of the reading is shared with the pupils. When reading *Holes* by Louis Sachar, pupils are assigned character parts to read (there are plenty), while others share narration. Pupils clamour to read their parts – it's lovely.

While reading Michael Morpurgo's *War Horse* with a tricky Year 9 class, they subdivided into small reading groups, having settled on a set of rules they wanted to follow, and blossomed into much more confident readers. This strategy also enables you to float around the class, pausing to pose questions to check levels of understanding. The class's reaction to the text, along with the mix of personalities and abilities,

will help you to decide the best method for sharing a class reader.

5 Pupils' reading habits. This can be the biggest limitation for all pupils in your class. Some pupils you teach won't even own a book (even on a tablet computer), can't, don't or won't read at home, and will barely read in school. If you don't give them the opportunity to read, to use the library, to share your passion for reading with them, who will?

6 The point about reading leads me on to vocabulary. Rather than a limited imagination, it is the limited vocabulary of your pupils that can hinder reading, writing, and speaking and listening. It hinders their ability to articulate themselves. How can we help?

■ Don't assume lower ability classes will enjoy easier-to-read texts. I had a low ability Year 8 class who thrived on the challenging language of Dickens and felt

'babied' by Roald Dahl's *Revolting Rhymes*.

- Get pupils to pick out the words they don't know from a text, get those dictionaries out, and then ask the pupils to use the new words in a different context or a context more relevant to them.

- Put a challenging text into Wordle. See what meaning they can make from the word cloud, and then get them to choose a number of words to use in a short burst of focused writing.

- Use thesauri combined with paint colour charts from a DIY shop. Pupils will need to consider the intensity of the words before matching them to the colour hue on a colour chart. (Not my idea – this was stolen from a Twitter colleague: @GoldfishBowlMM. He also writes very eloquently about his stages of teaching new vocabulary, brilliant.)

- Use images. Images are a vocabulary bank in picture form and are particularly helpful for EAL pupils.

7 Shakespeare. Alongside teaching novels, Shakespeare is the time when English teachers come most alive in an 'O Captain! My Captain' kind of way, but there's no getting around the fact that the language can be a barrier.

Start with a Shakespearean insults generator and have a ball spending a lesson insulting each other Shakespeare style! Get the pupils to write a short sketch of an argument using Shakespearean insults instead of swear words and you've cracked the language barrier, while focusing on the text as a drama. Bingo!

Use Shakespeare's Globe as a primary means of exploring the historical and social context. (@Xris32 has written an excellent post about this – how students were 'in role' as a Shakespearean audience, exploring how they would react to the content of the play and why.) The bareness of the Globe's stage also helps you explain why

Shakespeare has too many words – the set design is in Shakespeare's choice of imagery. Focus on the characters using action, reaction, dialogue and description. If pupils can understand characters' actions, their understanding of the plot falls into place.

It is a *play*, a three-dimensional text, which gives you masses of scope for creativity. Use drama, get pupils to direct each other, get them to direct you once you've done a deliberately awful performance of a character and, yes, use the good films available. Stage directions are also present within the language, so get pupils to dig it out.

Most importantly, don't be 'scatter gun'. There is always an assessment attached to the study of a Shakespeare text, so use that to plan and work backwards from. Even more importantly, be unashamed in your geeky enthusiasm for Shakespeare.

8 So, who *hasn't* marked a book with barely discernible handwriting? Nope, didn't think so. Sometimes this is down to rushing, carelessness, lack of motivation, any number of things. However, some pupils just have awful handwriting. It is important for them to write less but with greater accuracy. I've adapted @LearningSpy's idea of 'Slow Writing' specifically for these types of pupils and get them to write double spaced. This slows the pupils down and makes them take notice of the quality and accuracy of their work. It makes both teacher and peer marking much more helpful and effective for these pupils. Progress may be slow, but it is still progress.

9 Marking. I couldn't put it off forever. Here are some suggestions:

- Peer marking. Pupils need training and practice at this before it is anywhere near useful to them. A success criterion using traffic lights can be useful. Give a very specific success criterion (e.g. only focusing on sentence structure or use of connectives). Make this a dialogue between you and your pupils.

- Peer critique. Show Ron Berger's 'The Story of Austin's Butterfly' from YouTube, discuss its purpose, what it achieves and stick to the 'kind, fair and specific' rule. Provide some precise success criteria, which could also be negotiated with pupils, and off you go.

- My handwriting is awful, so I started using symbols for my literacy marking (e.g. a triangle for a punctuation error, squiggly underline for a misused or misplaced word). But I didn't tell the pupils what the symbols meant – they had to work them out. I think I stole this from @JamesTheo – thanks James! They had to focus on the frequency of certain symbols to work out their most common errors and use this to set targets for the next piece of writing.

- A taxonomy of errors. This idea is from @kevbartle and @amsammons. When marking books or essays, keep a track of common errors in the group. Sort these into easy, medium and hard fixes, then get pupils to read through their work and find their own common errors and set their own targets. Make sure pupils have time to respond to and act on advice given – often called Directed Improvement and Reflection Time (DIRT).[1]

■ Devise a marking rota for your classes and mark little and often. Having said that, it is the Holy Grail of all English teachers to manage marking better. Answers on a postcard please …

10 When setting pupils a writing task, do the task too. This has a range of benefits. If you are busy writing, they cannot fall back on the 'I don't get it' cop-out. The pupils just have to have a go and crack on with it. You place yourself in the same boat as the pupils. They will see you stopping to think, scribble things out and maybe not even complete it. This is a normal part of writing.

place yourself in the same boat as the pupils

You are as vulnerable as they are when it comes to sharing work with the class, so tell them so. The first time I did this it was a practice essay for a WJEC Lang/Lit comparing two poems in one hour. It is *tough*. I was terrified that what I produced might be rubbish. I shared it with my lovely girls' class who were brilliant – they saw my fear. They were then more willing to celebrate each other's successes and more supportive of each other's difficulties with writing.

Celebrate the pupils' writing in class as much as you can. One Year 7 class were keen to read out their work when they could hold my special cuddly toy 'Ben Banana' (thank you Co-op). I think it worked because the toy was comforting and made them feel special. They had also been 'trained' in peer critique so could offer constructive feedback in each other's work, some resulting in spontaneous applause.

Peer critique also promotes a positive attitude to redrafting and that it's perfectly acceptable for the first effort to be not 'good enough yet', and that the second and third attempts will each be better constructed, not just neater.

1 See J. Beere, *The Perfect (Ofsted) Lesson*, rev. edn (Carmarthen: Independent Thinking Press, 2012).

Get to know your students ...
what they like and don't like
... having an understanding of
your students will help you
to engage *all* students

SPORT AND PE

MATHEW PULLEN @MAT6453

1 Be diverse. Don't try to be the expert in all sports. Let students see that you are human and that they can teach you new things. It will engage them and help to build great relationships.

2 Get an iPad. They are essential in PE to help students analyse performance – they can take PE to the next level of performance analysis. Apps like Ubersense, Coach's Eye and CoachNote are great tools to help students make sense of activities.

3 Don't isolate yourself in the PE department. There are so many great things going on in schools that you need to make sure you see it happening.

4 Set up cross-curricular projects. Maths and science lend themselves well to working with sport. In this way, students will see the relevance of subjects beyond the subjects themselves.

5 Be available to support others. Teaching is a hard game and it is essential that staff support each other. For sport it is especially hard on cold and wet winter days, so make sure you take time to check in on colleagues.

6 Read, read, read and then read some more. There are so many great teachers around and they are doing great things. Many fantastic teachers write blogs and share what they are doing. This is invaluable.

7 Join Twitter and follow @ PEgeeks. This is where many PE teachers post ideas and have terrific discussions about PE – you will learn a lot.

8 Start your own blog. It is a good way to document your own development and to see the impact you are having. You don't need to publish it publicly but it is a good step to take eventually. All you need to do is write down the things you are trying and the difference it is making.

9 Be brave and try new things. Sometimes it may feel safe to just keep traditional and do things how they have always been done. But this leads to a lack of engagement. Students will appreciate you trying out new things and it shows that you are attempting to deliver a great experience to students.

10 Get to know your students. Not just names, but what they like and don't like, the things they do outside of school. Like it or not, not everyone will love sport as much as you, so having an understanding of your students will help you to engage *all* students in lessons, and not just the obviously sporty ones.

WORKING WITH SEN CHILDREN IN A MAINSTREAM SETTING

AMY HARVEY @MS_JAMDANGORY

For a teacher, there is nothing better than the moment when a child's understanding clicks, **other than that moment for a child with SEN.**

1 Make sure all staff understand the child's needs and abilities, and try to match staff with SEN children appropriately.

2 Include the child in as much of the normal school day as possible and differentiate activities so they can work alongside other children. This lets the rest of class know they are a classmate.

3 Write smart individual education plans that the child can understand and can achieve quickly, then do another one, and so on.

4 Build a great relationship with the parents. Remember that to them their child is the most important child in your class. Make them feel like that is true.

5 Get iPads, especially for children who have attention and fine motor difficulties. Quick and improved results will happen and will make the child achieve success, and smile!

33

6   Help the child to become independent in the classroom as far as possible. Give them their own set of equipment and easy access to reading books so they can change books and so on themselves.

7   Make the child laugh. Build a trusting relationship with them so they enjoy coming to school.

8   Have good relationships with external agencies so they *want* to come into your school and help your children, and will pop in when they have time.

9   Be firm with the children – they too need to understand and follow school rules. It will help them in the big bad world.

10 Love them. They are delightful, different and demanding. But aren't we all? For a teacher, there is nothing better than the moment when a child's understanding clicks, other than that moment for a child with SEN.

QUESTIONING STRATEGIES

ALEX QUIGLEY @HUNTINGENGLISH

> Learn from yesterday, live for today, hope for tomorrow. The important thing is to not stop questioning.
>
> **Albert Einstein**

Most research indicates that as much as 80% of classroom questioning is based on low order, factual, recall questions. We must put questioning back at the centre of our pedagogy and planning. We need to create a culture of enquiry and engagement in high quality, high order questioning if formative progress is to be identified effectively.

1 Key questions as learning objectives. What better way to foster a culture of enquiry than to spark the whole shooting match off with a big question that gets students thinking critically about what they are going to learn? By asking a big question you can initiate thinking and group discussion that immediately engages students in their prospective learning. By framing it as a question it can raise motivation, as students feel like they have invested choice in their learning. And by getting students to subsequently formulate the learning objective, they really begin to think about the nuances of what they are to learn and why.

2 'If this is the answer ... what is the question?' This simple little technique, taken from the show *Mock the Week*, sparks inquisitiveness in students. Just by quickly reversing the standard question-and-answer dichotomy it can deepen their thinking. It could be a relatively closed answer, like '3.14159265359' (the numerical value of pi) or something more open, like 'religion'.

3 Thunks®. These little gems are great for initiating deeper thinking, with seemingly simple questions opening up a complex array of higher order thinking. Thunks like, 'If I ask if I can steal your pen and you say yes, is that stealing?' or, 'Can I ever step on the same beach twice?' are great fun and thoughtful starters. These clever questions (see Ian Gilbert's excellent

The Little Book of Thunks[1] or the website www.thunks.co.uk) can simply be used to spark thinking or dialogue, or they can be more targeted towards the topic or subject at hand. As the students become familiar with thunking (in my experience they really enjoy it), they can begin to formulate their own thunks – a great way to get them to think about higher order, open questioning.

4 'Just one more question … ' Given any topic or subject, the students have to work collaboratively in groups to create an array of quality questions. They can then be given a series of challenging question stems to broaden their range of questions, using the following question stems: 'What if … ?', 'Suppose we knew … ?' and 'What would change if … ?' If they write the questions on sticky notes they can then be collated and saved – with the teacher returning to them further down the learning line. As the topic develops students can add 'just one more question', as well as answering the initial questions as their understanding grows. By following this method, you can continue to foster the crucial culture of enquiry in the classroom – encouraging questions as a matter of course. Generating a range of such questions is a great way to initiate a topic because it helps to highlight miscomprehension immediately. It

Pose, pause, bounce, pounce

can also foster collaboration and it can give the teacher precise and immediate, formative feedback to shape their subsequent planning for the topic.

5 Questioning monitor. This technique constructively involves students in the evaluation and reflection of the questioning process. A monitor, or a pair of monitors, would be given the responsibility for tracking and monitoring the frequency of questions – teacher or student, open or closed, factual or conceptual. You can have them monitor for a given task or gather more cumulative research by extending it over a week or two of lessons. By exploring the evidence you are signalling to the students that you value evidence. You are also diagnosing the quality of your own questioning and that of the students. You will then have the evidence to know whether you really have a culture of enquiry – and, if not, what steps you need to take to develop one. The activity sends very powerful messages to students about how highly you value quality questioning.

6 Socratic questioning and Socratic circles. The old dog really can teach us new tricks! Socrates believed that questioning was at the root of all learning – and it is hard to disagree. The six steps of Socratic questioning create a critical atmosphere that probes thinking and once more gets the students questioning in a structured way. There are six main categories:

---

1 I. Gilbert, *The Little Book of Thunks: 260 questions to make your brain go ouch* (Carmarthen: Crown House Publishing, 2007).

Q1 Get your students to clarify their thinking, for instance: 'Why do you say that?', 'Could you explain that further?'

Q2 Challenging students about assumptions, for instance: 'Is this always the case?', 'Why do you think that this assumption holds here?'

Q3 Evidence as a basis for argument questions, such as: 'Why do you say that?', 'Is there reason to doubt this evidence?'

Q4 Viewpoints and perspectives. This challenges the students to investigate other ways of looking at the same issue, for instance: 'What is the counter-argument for ... ?', 'Can/Did anyone see this another way?'

Q5 Implications and consequences. Given that actions have consequences, this is an area ripe for questioning, for instance: 'But if that happened, what else would result?', 'How does ... affect ... ?' By investigating this, students may analyse more carefully before jumping to an opinion.

Q6 Question the question. Just when students think they have a valid answer, this is where you can tip them back into the pit, for instance: 'Why do you think I asked that question?', 'Why was that question important?'

The 'Socratic circles' strategy is a great way to strategically organise such questioning involving the whole group – see http://www.corndancer.com/tunes/tunes_print/soccirc.pdf/.

7 Pose, pause, bounce, pounce.[2] This is a brilliantly simple but very important strategy. The thinking time at the 'pause' point is crucial – there is a great deal of evidence about how the quality of responses and the confidence levels of students is raised by even a short amount of thinking time. The 'bounce' is also essential in that, once again, students are expected to constructively build on the ideas of one another, which gets them focused on a consistent basis when trained.

8 Question continuum.[3] The continuum involves the students first devising questions, in pairs or groups, on any given topic or idea. Then the continuum is created very visibly, either on the whiteboard or semi-permanently on a display board (which can be great for resuming the strategy in future lessons), with student questions written on sticky notes for added flexibility. The horizontal axis would represent the 'interest level' generated by each question – that is, how likely the question is to inspire new thinking and new possibilities. The vertical axis could be flexible in a variety of ways, should you wish to include a vertical axis. For example, it could represent 'complexity' (from 'closed factual questions' to 'open conceptual questions'). Students could feed back their opinions, shaped by the teacher, to identify

2 For more on this strategy see: C. Harrison and S. Howard, *Inside the Primary Black Box: Assessment for Learning in Primary and Early Years Classrooms* (London: GL Assessment, 2009).

3 J. Beere, *The Perfect (Ofsted) Lesson* (Carmarthen: Crown House Publishing, 2012).

the best questions – which then could be the subject of further exploration. Having the questions very visible means you can also flexibly rearrange them, such as selecting the 'best' nine questions and creating a new 'diamond nine' formation.

9 The question wall (a design upgrade for a well-used technique). With regards to pedagogy, the question continuum clearly overlaps with the question wall, so I would be wary of trying both concurrently with groups so as not to confuse them. The question wall, in this instance, is a working space for students to communicate questions about their learning. Giving students sticky notes and asking them to write down their questions typically eliminates those questions that reflect 'learned helplessness' – the, 'How do you spell such and such?' when they have a dictionary, or, 'What do we have to do?' in response to your lengthy and erudite explanation of the task at hand. To add a level of nuance to the wall, consider creating simple sections with labels – for example, closed questions are placed on the left-hand side of the wall and more open questions are placed progressively to the right-hand side.

10 Hinge point questions. These questions are simple, closed questions which give you immediate feedback on student understanding but which may determine a 'hinge point' shift in the direction of the learning – for example, they may highlight that you need to revisit certain aspects. It is handy to colour code these key questions in your lesson plan, with the aim of creating genuine flexibility in your planning.

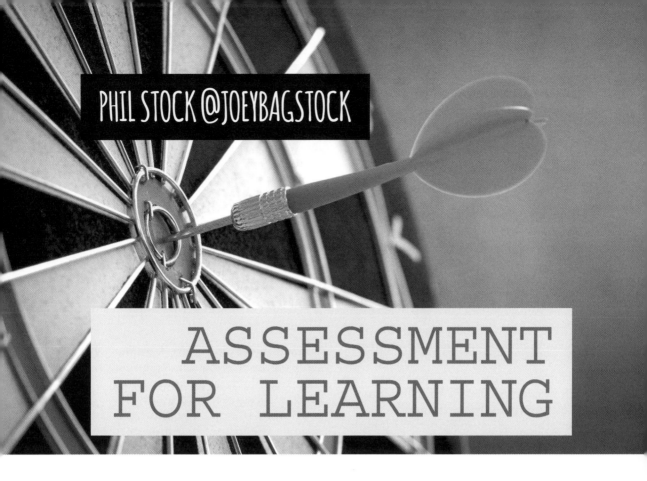

PHIL STOCK @JOEYBAGSTOCK

ASSESSMENT FOR LEARNING

We all know what we want our students to learn, what we want them to understand and be able to do at the end of each term, year or course. Determining where students are in relation to these learning goals, and what they need to do in order to move closer towards them, is often rather more problematic.

Accurately observing students' learning is difficult: not only does learning take place over a much longer period of time than one lesson, but it also remains hidden from our view. While we want to make the process of learning visible for students, knowing exactly whether they have really learned what we want them to learn is harder to make transparent. Often when we are making judgements about students' progress we are evaluating their present performance. Come back tomorrow or next lesson and we may sometimes find that the learning we thought was secure is not.

Therefore, we need to make sure that the ways in which we assess the progress of our students is as reliable and instructive as possible. We want, as much as possible, to make sure that the information we have is accurate and that it genuinely helps inform our subsequent teaching. To this end, there is not really one perfect means of assessing students' learning, but rather an array of methods that help give us the data we need to plan for our students' progression.

Good teachers naturally use and vary their approaches to assessment in order to maximise the quality of information they receive. Here are ten simple methods of assessing student progress, along with some links to more detailed wider reading about their practical application and benefits.

1   HINGE QUESTIONS

These are essentially questions you pose to a class at a crucial point in their learning in order to determine where they are at and how you should proceed with your teaching. You are really trying to gauge whether a given idea, factual detail or skill has been understood so that you can build on it with your subsequent instruction. A hinge question can come at any point in a lesson because it is really about students' progress across a teaching sequence rather than within a specific lesson. The questions themselves are usually in a multiple-choice format, since these are easy to administer and, more importantly, the results from students can be processed quickly and effectively. A good hinge question takes quite a lot of planning because you are essentially aiming to use their incorrect answers to give you formative information: you want to understand the misconceptions that students have about relevant aspects of their learning. To write a question with four plausible answers, but ultimately only one correct one, is quite an art and takes considerable practice. It might be worth working

collaboratively with colleagues on good hinge questions. Once you have the questions they can be recycled in the future.

http://improvingteaching.co.uk/2013/08/17/hinge-questions-in-history/?relatedposts_exclude=651/

http://improvingteaching.co.uk/2013/11/03/oiling-the-hinges-refining-my-construction-of-hinge-question/

2   MULTIPLE CHOICE ASSESSMENTS

Some subjects are more familiar with using multiple choice questions as a reliable means of assessing student progress than others. Indeed, in subjects like maths and science the format has proven to be a relatively quick and easy means of checking certain types of knowledge and understanding. Other more essay-based subjects, such as English and history, may not initially appear to be able to take advantage of multiple choice questions as a valid form of assessment. However, this is not the case. Multiple choice can be a very useful and efficient method of assessment across a range of subjects, if the questions are structured in the right way and they are assessing the right kinds of material. As with the workings of the hinge format, good questions in longer multiple choice assessments aim to see whether students have arrived at any misconceptions in their learning. Four or five choices is considered to be the ideal number of options, all of which need to be plausible responses and have an underlying rationale to them. It is as much about the wrong answers as it is about the right answers. There are a number of apps that can help you to administer multiple choice assessments and programs like Flubaroo can help to analyse the results efficiently.

http://joeybagstock.wordpress.com/2013/11/20/is-there-a-place-for-multiple-choice-in-english-part-i/

http://joeybagstock.wordpress.com/2013/11/29/there-is-a-place-for-multiple-choice-in-english-part-ii-2/

3 QUESTIONING

This is the bread and butter of teaching. Questioning remains one of the most reliable and simplest ways to assess understanding, although there are a number of things to be aware of in making sure that you ask the right questions of the right students. While there is a time and place for closed questions (note: not for behaviour management purposes) more open-ended questions are better ways of gauging students' understanding. To this end, you might find it advisable to plan the kinds of questions you are going to ask during the lesson to check understanding and at what points you intend to ask them, particularly if you are teaching a difficult topic for the first time.

While some people like to use random generators (such as lollipop sticks or computer programs), in many respects it might be more advisable to target the students yourself for the purpose of assessing their understanding. As you get to know a class, you will be able to select individuals who you suspect may be struggling or choose certain students to act as a guide for whole-class understanding. The pose, pause, bounce, pounce method is an effective way of engaging multiple students in the assessment process and building a more nuanced picture of different levels of understanding within a mixed ability classroom.[1] Asking increasingly complex questions also helps to develop understanding. In the hands of a skilful practitioner, questioning can help to move students on in their learning using what they already know.

http://www.scoop.it/t/effective-questioning-in-the-classroom/

4 MINI WHITEBOARDS

These are sometimes given a hard time by those who question their efficacy in the classroom, particularly the disruption they can sometimes cause and the time wasted in getting their usage properly organised. These arguments can be countered by making sure that your classes are well drilled in getting them out, using them correctly and putting them away again. Time spent early in the autumn term helping to get students used to routines like these can pay dividends later on in the year when you can use them to gauge students' understanding quickly and effectively.

Whiteboards can be used in conjunction with hinge questions to check students' responses to multiple choice questions or simply

---

1 For more on this strategy, see C. Harrison and S. Howard, *Inside the Primary Black Box: Assessment for Learning in Primary and Early Years Classrooms* (London: GL Assessment, 2009), p. 15.

to check different aspects of student understanding throughout a lesson or lessons. For example, students could write out the spelling of a key word, an important date or, if the board is one of the bigger ones, a brief explanation following a framing cue from the teacher. As with all methods of assessment, students need to be familiar with what is expected of them, the teacher has to be clear what they are looking for (remember, wrong answers are just as instructive as right ones) and the results have to be able to be interpreted efficiently.

5   EXIT TICKETS

These are a means of assessing what students have learned during a lesson. They are essentially pieces of paper that students give to the teacher as they leave the classroom which show the teacher whether what was taught that lesson was understood or not. An exit ticket can be in a multiple-choice format or, better still, use one or two straightforward open questions that the students can give a quick response to in order to demonstrate their learning. After the lesson, the teacher uses the results from the exit tickets to inform their planning for the next lesson.

http://back2thewhiteboard.wordpress.com/2012/06/22/117/

6   STICKY NOTES

This is a slight variation on the exit ticket model. Here students write down questions that they have about the lesson, topic or unit and place them on the wall or the whiteboard on their way out. It is usually a good idea to give students some idea of the kind of information that they

could provide you with in their questions as you want to make sure that the feedback will help you to assess their understanding so that you can act on it.

7   MARKING BOOKS DURING THE LESSON

Perhaps this is so obvious that it is not really worth mentioning, but we should not forget the value of cruising around the room (a Bill Rogers' phrase that I have always loved), peering over students' shoulders and gleaning information about their levels of understanding. Depending on the class and the circumstances, it is possible to get a decent overview of a group or individual's learning and to provide decent, formative feedback that they can act on straight away.

http://reflectingenglish.wordpress.com/2013/12/21/differentiating-the-responsive-way/

8   MARKING BOOKS AFTER THE LESSON

Along with questioning, marking the work students produce is one of the most important and fundamental aspects of teaching. The problem is that it's very time consuming to do in detail and on a regular basis. For too long a great deal of our marking has not been read by the students or acted on in any meaningful way. Yet marking a class set of books remains one of the most powerful ways to check understanding, particularly when students are bringing together different facets of their learning in an extended response. Keep a notepad with you when you mark a set of books and jot down a list of frequent errors or misconceptions and use these details to inform your future planning. Remember: marking is planning.

http://www.scoop.it/t/useoffeedback/

9   SELF-ASSESSMENT

Self-assessment and peer assessment (see tip number 10) were one of the main aspects of the recommendations for implementing AfL in the classroom.[2] They both operate on the premise that students are taking greater ownership over their learning by understanding the criteria for assessment and evaluating their own work in light of this understanding. Done badly, self-assessment can be reduced to a simple box-ticking exercise or class filler with little learning taking place. Done well, it can be a powerful way for students to set their own targets and become more successful learners, who are able to reflect on their own strengths and weaknesses and make improvements accordingly.

In order to help make self-assessment more effective, it is wise to use the technique towards the end of a cycle of learning (i.e. at the end of a unit or teaching sequence) rather than after every piece of work. To state the obvious:

2 D. Wiliam, C. Lee, C. Harrison and P. Black, 'Teachers developing assessment for learning: impact on student achievement', *Assessment in Education: Principles Policy and Practice* 11(1) (2004): 49–65 OR P. Black, C. Harrison, C. Lee, B. Marshall and D. Wiliam, *Assessment for Learning: Putting It Into Practice* (Buckingham: Open University Press, 2003.)

students need to fully understand what the criteria they are being assessed on actually mean, otherwise their comments tend to be misguided or rather too simplistic. This takes time and carefully structured coaching.

10   PEER ASSESSMENT

This works along the same lines as self-assessment. Students need to understand the criteria properly and be given sufficient time to evaluate the work properly. The key to successful peer assessment is the choice of students who work together in pairs or small groups. This is where the teacher's knowledge of their class comes into its own. Sometimes students of a similar ability assessing each other's work can prove effective, while there are also occasions when a more able student, or students, paired with less able students can work well. The more able student has to know how to explain improvement steps to the less able student, while the less able student sees an authentic example of successful work and works with a peer to understand the reasons for its success.

TECHNOLOGIES TO PROMOTE CREATIVE LEARNING

Teachers are constantly searching for new ways to promote good learning. If those ways can also encourage creative thinking then they are even more welcome in the classroom. Technology can provide some of those creative solutions. Here are five ideas for using technology to support learning while promoting creative thinking. I'm sure that with a little thought you will be able to adapt them to your own subject area.

STEVE WHEELER @TIMBUCKTEETH

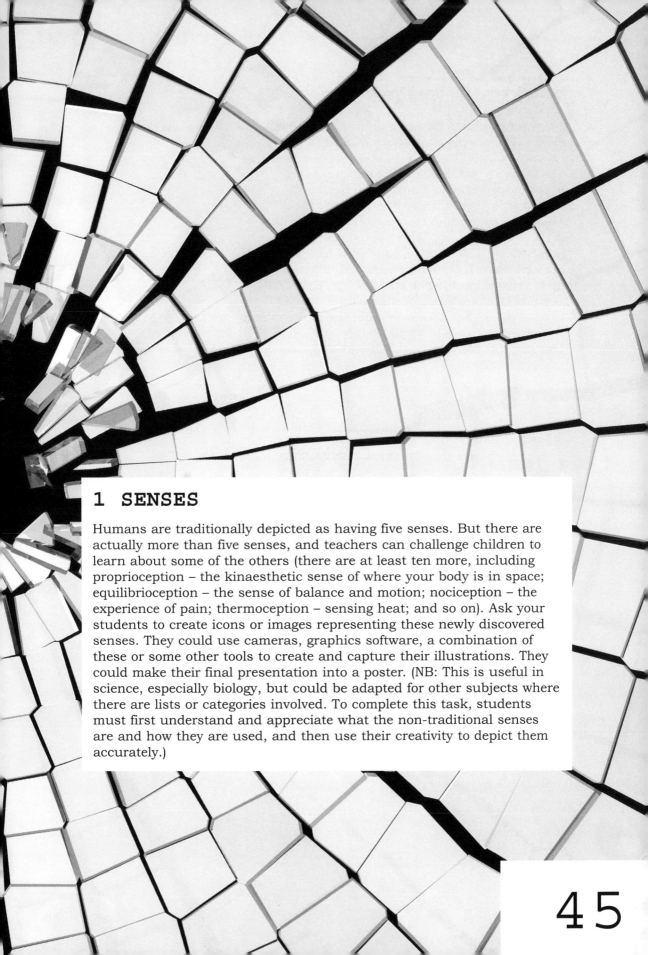

1 SENSES

Humans are traditionally depicted as having five senses. But there are actually more than five senses, and teachers can challenge children to learn about some of the others (there are at least ten more, including proprioception – the kinaesthetic sense of where your body is in space; equilibrioception – the sense of balance and motion; nociception – the experience of pain; thermoception – sensing heat; and so on). Ask your students to create icons or images representing these newly discovered senses. They could use cameras, graphics software, a combination of these or some other tools to create and capture their illustrations. They could make their final presentation into a poster. (NB: This is useful in science, especially biology, but could be adapted for other subjects where there are lists or categories involved. To complete this task, students must first understand and appreciate what the non-traditional senses are and how they are used, and then use their creativity to depict them accurately.)

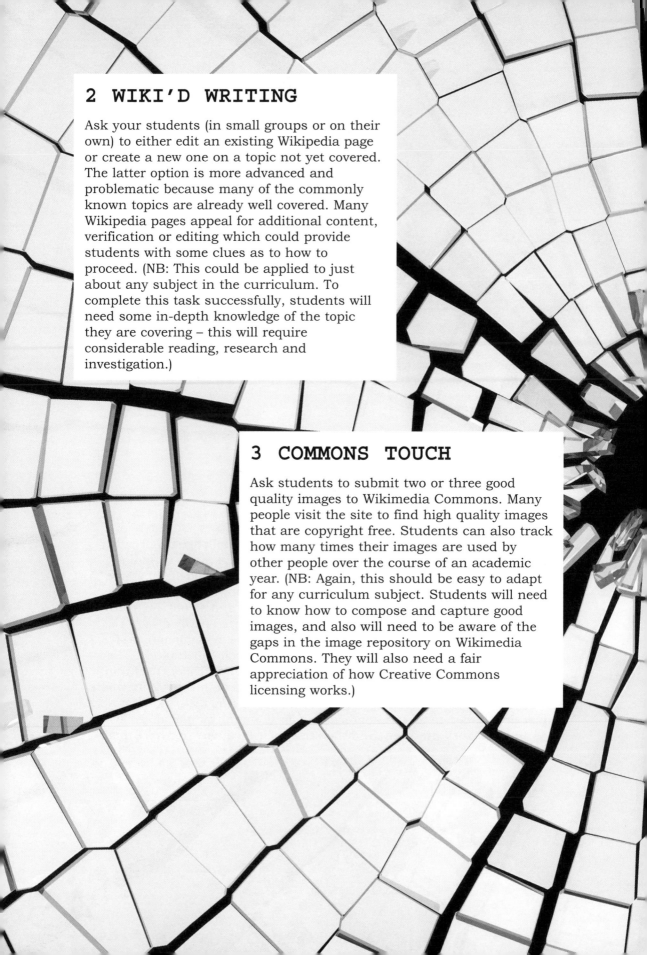

2 WIKI'D WRITING

Ask your students (in small groups or on their own) to either edit an existing Wikipedia page or create a new one on a topic not yet covered. The latter option is more advanced and problematic because many of the commonly known topics are already well covered. Many Wikipedia pages appeal for additional content, verification or editing which could provide students with some clues as to how to proceed. (NB: This could be applied to just about any subject in the curriculum. To complete this task successfully, students will need some in-depth knowledge of the topic they are covering – this will require considerable reading, research and investigation.)

3 COMMONS TOUCH

Ask students to submit two or three good quality images to Wikimedia Commons. Many people visit the site to find high quality images that are copyright free. Students can also track how many times their images are used by other people over the course of an academic year. (NB: Again, this should be easy to adapt for any curriculum subject. Students will need to know how to compose and capture good images, and also will need to be aware of the gaps in the image repository on Wikimedia Commons. They will also need a fair appreciation of how Creative Commons licensing works.)

4 MAKING TWISTORY

Get students to follow, and interact with, historical figures on Twitter. What kind of questions should they ask? How might they get the historical figures to respond to their questions? There are many characters to choose from, such as William Shakespeare, Florence Nightingale, Benjamin Franklin and Henry VIII. If you would like to have a go at tweeting as a historical character yourself, here's a link showing you how to be a historical figure on Twitter. http://seanmunger. com/2011/03/10/how-to-be-a-historical-figure-on-twitter-a-few-tips/ (NB: This is great for the study of history, but could be adapted to English language and literature (authors), science or technology (scientists and inventors), geography (explorers) and foreign languages (tweets in those languages – see also Lingua Tweeta)). Students will need to search for and verify celebrity or historical figure Twitter accounts and then frame the questions they wish to ask them.)

5 VIDEO MASH-UPS

Ask students to find three unrelated YouTube videos. Using the built-in YouTube editor, ask them to select sections and mash them up, mixing elements to create a totally new message. How is the message different to those of the three component videos used? What does the message mean now, and how does the sequence of moving images and/or narrative support that message (form)? Who is the mash-up video aimed at (audience and purpose)? (NB: This is ideal for English language or media teaching, but could be adapted to other subject areas. Your students will need to know about purpose, audience and form, they will need to understand how to compare and contrast, and they will also need to learn how to use the YouTube editing tools.)

SOLO TAXONOMY

ANDREW DAY @ANDYPHILIPDAY

1 Don't be intimidated by the terms of SOLO taxonomy. So, the phrase Structure of Observed Learning Outcomes doesn't roll off the tongue, but it does sequence progression and define conceptual sophistication in a way that both teacher and student can readily adopt. It moves learning from a zone of unknowing (prestructural) to acquiring one valid piece of relevant information (unistructural), accruing a breadth of knowledge and information (multistructural), identifying patterns among the information (relational) before being creative with the deeper learning (extended abstract).

2 Read the blogs of those who have used SOLO. Not everyone finds it a useful taxonomy for their teaching. But there are thousands of teachers out there who do – and of a wide age-range of student (from teachers of primary to post-graduate level) and of most subject areas (from performance subjects to those that have a significant amount of knowledge content). There are schools using SOLO taxonomy as an institution-wide vehicle for excellence. One such is St Mary's College in Blackpool, led by Stephen Tierney. His blog is worth reading for his SOLO posts: http://leadinglearner. me/2013/04/14/redesigning-classrooms-using-solo-to-increase-challenge/.

3 If you are uncertain about where to start using SOLO, start with your lesson plan. I often read of teachers having absorbed lots of information on SOLO but who are unsure how to start using it in a lesson. Practise with your learning objectives. When you plan your lessons, select a mix of 'shallow learning' outcomes (unistructural and multistructural) but go on to the 'deeper learning' ones too (relational and extended abstract). Don't feel every lesson has to include all four of the conceptual stages, but make sure there is at least one shallow and one deeper learning outcome. The students don't need to know the terms (or even that you're using SOLO), but build up your familiarity with the concepts and how they frame the learning in your subject.

4 Use SOLO to differentiate the learning activities of a lesson. Some teachers have found value in setting up groups of desks in SOLO workstations with activities dedicated to each of the four active SOLO stages. Alternatively, different levels of SOLO tasks can be put in a grid on a whiteboard with students opting for, or being directed to, the most appropriate starting position. Whichever stage students begin at, check they are able to access the necessary information and knowledge to be able to work with it creatively in the relational and extended abstract stages.

5 Encourage students to aim for depth and quality at each stage. Some students will try to rush through each of the SOLO stages to get to a perceived goal of ticking off the 'extended abstract' level. It's not a race, and this misses the point that the deeper learning stages assume, at their heart, that students

49

have accrued a broad range of relevant and rich knowledge. In the old computer-programming adage, 'Garbage in, garbage out'. At the unistructural stage, check that the key information has precision, and at the multistructural stage, test the breadth and depth of age-appropriate material for the deep learning manipulation to which it will be subjected in the relational and extended abstract stages.

6 Frame the actions and language that students will require to explore the SOLO stages. Your reading on SOLO won't go far without you coming across hexagons. This is just one technique to help students record and accumulate key information (multistructural) and encourage flexible associations, depending on whether you want students to sequence, classify, sort or identify cause and/or effect (all relational). Venn diagrams can achieve a similar end when a 'compare and contrast' activity is called for. As for the language of each stage, consider providing a SOLO taxonomy wordmat to facilitate fluency at each stage (e.g. https://www.dropbox.com/s/emjscllglgdveox/SOLO%20taxonomy%20wordmat.docx).

7 Assist students to see where they are on their progress path. Check students understand the conceptual stage they are at, and where they should proceed next, by providing opportunities for them to self- (or peer) assess their work. Having made explicit, and exemplified, what work looks like at each of the four active SOLO stages, encourage students – via highlighters, sticky notes, symbol-fobs and/or graded mark schemes – to identify what stage a particular response has attained and what is required for it to be moved to the next stage. Develop their ability to consider it through the eyes of an assessor.

8 Frame your questioning through the lens of SOLO stages. The mark of a high-performing classroom is frequently demonstrated by the quality of student questioning (and responses) which conveys the learning ethos. Too often, teacher questions focus on shallow learning to the exclusion of richer areas. Frame your questions to specific individuals using the full range of SOLO stages. Check the solidity of the knowledge (unistructural) and the breadth and depth of it (multistructural), but challenge students to seek patterns and connect the information (relational) and use the ideas generated to forecast, hypothesise, predict and synthesise (extended abstract).

> The mark of a high-performing classroom is frequently demonstrated by the quality of student questioning (and responses)

9 Develop your curriculum design through the SOLO hierarchy. Define your subject-specific progress criteria by considering the key attributes of top-performing

students in age-related assessment tasks. Whether these are public examinations, internal tests or individual units of work, specify the dexterity of thought and conceptual reach you expect high achievers to be able to demonstrate. Establish which attributes of the extended abstract stage are required and then reverse engineer. Work back through the relational attributes students need to operate, and the degree of precision, depth and breadth of knowledge/information by which the competency is demonstrated.

10 Play with SOLO. The taxonomy is one among many. It's not an add-on, bolt-on or silver bullet. It doesn't make children behave (although I've noticed it can assist with engagement). Use it – in part or in full. Select that which you think can help you answer a problem or resolve an issue that nothing else yet has. Don't revere it. Play around with it. Be selective, judicious, try it with some groups but not others. Make it work for you and see where you can take it. If it helps to clarify the progress criteria for your subject, structure your teaching or illuminate your students' learning to them, then it will more than pay back any investment of your time in reading about it.

ART

PETE JONES @PEKABELO

Celebrate the artist.
Never does a week go by when
students fail to amaze me with
their artistic brilliance.

1   Teach Year 7s like they belong in the sixth form. I
    believe the quicker you give students the skills and
    knowledge to become artistically intelligent, the more
    likely they will grasp the mantle of artistic
    brilliance. How do artists work? Do they spend an
    hour a week doing 'bits and pieces which develop into
    a project' or do they spend hours thinking things
    through and making careful decisions? Providing the
    conditions for the latter has made a profound
    difference to how my students approach art.

2   Critique. This is a wonderful tool to get students
    analysing and helping others to improve their work
    through the simple, yet incredibly effective, critique
    protocol of being 'kind, specific and helpful' when
    analysing another student's work. I always start a
    new class with a showing of 'The Story of Austin's
    Butterfly' to get the ball rolling: http://www.youtube.
    com/watch?v=hqh1MRWZjms/.

3   Exemplar work. Keep a folder of excellence to bring
    out when setting expectations for new learning.
    Demonstrate how this work is created, what conditions
    are needed, how long it takes, what might be the
    pitfalls and what to look out for if aiming for
    excellence. I always create examples of everything the
    students are expected to do. It really helps when you
    want to explain the process of creating work of
    excellence. Having a variety of examples, with common
    mistakes or different stages of the process, can be
    invaluable too.

4   Success criteria. Without this, students can be left
    blind to understanding the expectations of a project.
    I always say that the very highest level is there to
    be broken and that this is only a guideline to
    expectations. It's what you could do, not necessarily
    what you should do.

5   Flipped learning. Having only one art lesson a week
    in most of our schools at Key Stage 3 does mean that
    the time in the art room is incredibly precious for
    many of our students. Flipped learning allows students
    to be primed ready for your lesson so you can spend
    more time with the finer nuances of learning in the

classroom. Create video demonstrations, point out artists to look into and get students to look at your PowerPoint slides before the lesson. This will cut down on the time needed to go over things in lessons and optimise the time for creating.

6 Growth mindset. I used to get so bored of students telling me 'I can't draw!' Adding 'yet' to the end of that statement can have profound effects on student expectations of achievement. I truly believe everyone can paint, everyone can draw. It's about work ethic and self-belief. I have a whole load of tricks up my sleeve which allow students to access the traits of a growth mindset. You will need to build your own, but do it - it really does make a difference. Praising hard work, rather than talent, is a very good starting point.

7 Be critical. The last thing students want to hear is, 'Yeah, it's going well' or 'It's getting there', when it's not. Give students honest feedback about what's good, what's not, what they need to do to improve and why they aren't making progress with their work. As art teachers, we are in the enviable position that we see the learning happening immediately - the understanding, the skills developed, the mistakes. If something isn't quite right, do something about it. The only way we can stretch every student is by giving advice on how to move their work closer to excellence, step by step. If students are saying to you, 'Yeah, but you say everyone's work is brilliant', it may be time to change your patter.

8 Celebrate the artist. Never does a week go by when students fail to amaze me with their artistic brilliance. Do everything you can to ensure work of excellence doesn't go unnoticed. Exhibit publicly when you can, speak to parents, involve the community, share the passion of your department as widely as you can. This is what will create the buzz.

9 Make work challenging. Art is not a 'doss' subject where students come to 'express themselves'. They are here to overcome immense challenges and stretch their thinking beyond their own expectations. If you are

getting students to think, act, learn and work like artists, they will be suitably challenged. The work of an artist is one who is constantly making mistakes, stumbling, striving and occasionally thriving through a sea of relentless questioning. Is this your classroom?

10 The sketchbook. Treat a sketchbook as the Holy Grail of 'working out' books. I encourage my students to make every page in their books worthy of a best-selling page turner. It should be packed full of beautiful mistakes, complex questions and endless research. If everything they do is of excellence, where will they get to? Brings me back nicely to my first top tip!

Teach Year 7s like they belong in the sixth form.

I believe the quicker you give students the skills and knowledge to become artistically intelligent, the more likely they will grasp the mantle of artistic brilliance.

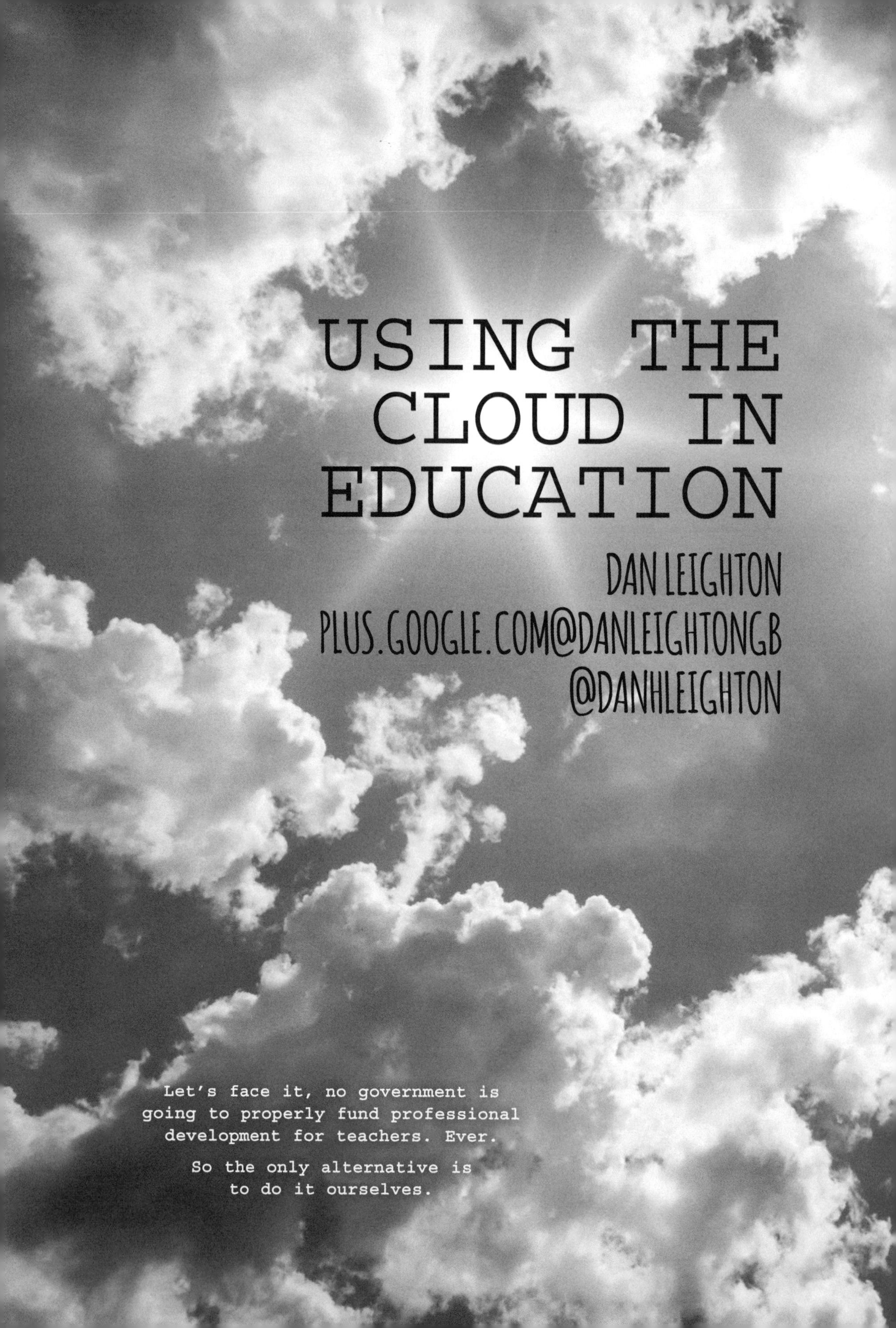

USING THE CLOUD IN EDUCATION

DAN LEIGHTON
PLUS.GOOGLE.COM@DANLEIGHTONGB
@DANHLEIGHTON

Let's face it, no government is
going to properly fund professional
development for teachers. Ever.

So the only alternative is
to do it ourselves.

1 Google+ is awesome for educational CPD. Let's face it, no government is going to properly fund professional development for teachers. Ever. So the only alternative is to do it ourselves. My number one tip for professionals wanting to improve their professional skills is this: install Google+ on your iOS or Android device. Once you've done that:

- 🛜 Join Google+.
- 🛜 Create a professional profile.
- 🛜 Create a circle called Educators and add everyone who looks interesting to it.
- 🛜 Join every community you can find which looks educational. Some of the big ones include Google Apps for Education, Chromebooks Edu, Chromebooks, Education Revolution and many more.

Once you have completed these steps, you will find that the stream in your Google+ app miraculously fills up with loads of cool and interesting things. +1 anything that looks appropriate and make the odd comment. The magic Google+ engine will then work out what you are interested in and feed you more of that stuff. I learn more from two or three minutes daily browsing of my Google+ stream than from whole day-long professional development courses. And it's not like Twitter. Most Google+ conversations are calm, measured and thoughtful. Professional, in other words. Inspiring.

2 Share everything. Think about it; as a teacher is there anything you will ever create that you will not, at some point, want to share with someone else? At which point, you might as well work in the cloud since you can then share everything seamlessly. Well, as long as you are using something like Google Apps for Education. You can try other systems but they are not in the same ballpark with respect to seamless collaboration yet, sorry. Schemes of learning, lesson plans, parent letters, lesson resources, test papers, quizzes, grading systems. Share it all.

3 Get students to do the assessment. We know that self-assessment and peer assessment are among the most effective things that a student can do to positively affect their learning (check out http://visible-learning.org/hattie-ranking-influences-effect-sizes-learning-achievement/). The trouble is that doing this offline, or even via email, involves multiple steps: setting work, waiting for it to be done, chasing late completers, printing, distributing, waiting for work to be done, chasing late completers, dealing with missing students, trying to find out who is late or incomplete, not being able to see the quality of work in progress. It can be never ending.

Here's the cloud alternative. Create a single document for all students to work on. Give them their own section within it. Share it with the class. All students work on it together and comment on each other's work. You watch the work appear in real time and chase up in class. Job done.

4 Get colleagues to do the work. Why would you want to send out an email attachment asking people for their comments on a document, wait for their reply and then have to go to all the trouble of collating the responses? Cloud version: share the single live document and ask them to make their changes to it. Use revision history to track edits if you need to.

5 Use comments on Google Docs and Slides as your number one teaching tool. Never mind all the whizzy EdTech stuff out there, all the hype about MOOCs (Massive Open Online Courses), the Khan Academy and all the rest. What makes the biggest difference to a student's learning (after they've gone to the trouble of actually thinking about their own understanding, cf. John Hattie, again) is for us teachers to comment on students' work and tell them how

to improve. Formative feedback, in UK educational jargon.

On a daily basis, my primary teaching tool for formative feedback is using comments on plain old Google Docs and Slides. These are like comments in Microsoft Word, but the student can see them as soon as you hit the enter key. My daily routine: share a doc or slide with the students containing the day's learning tasks, complete with spaces and titles for them to fill in (think worksheet); they do their work; I comment down the side in real time as they are working. This means they get the work correct earlier and with fewer misconceptions. They make faster progress as a consequence.

Think of it like this. We teachers are gardeners. We plant a knowledge seed in a lesson. We water it with a little information. Maybe dig in some manure to get things going a bit quicker and make it exciting. Then we wait while the student grows the seed. There are two alternative ways of gathering in the knowledge harvest.

Firstly, the traditional way of teaching, where we hand out books and wait for them to be handed back in for marking. In this way, we let the knowledge seed grow into a sapling, they tell us when they have finished growing it and we go along to look at their tree a while later. The tree is a bit bent over in the wrong direction and with a few extra branches here and there. We prune a bit off where they've misunderstood and put in a prop to get the tree growing straight and tall. This can all take a few days – if we are efficient and good professionals. And it's those few days which slow down the whole process and mean that the student has moved on from what they have written by the time they read the marking.

Alternatively, using our shared cloud-based doc or slide, we can watch as they actually type their work in real time. We can drop in our comments at the time of creation – and they can see them immediately. Because we can see what they are actually thinking in the moment of typing on our shared doc, we can guide them to grow the knowledge tree straight in the first place without any need for later props and pruning. Oh, and you have a record of all your marking, conveniently recorded next to the student's work when your department head, principal or friendly school inspector comes looking.

6 Bad behaviour is a behavioural issue, not a technology issue. If a student passes a rude note in class, do we ban paper and pens? Of course not! We deal with the bad behaviour through our normal behavioural systems. Likewise, if students are messing about on chat in a lesson, it's not the chat system's fault. They are behaving badly and the bad behaviour needs to be addressed in a manner identical to the normal systems. If you have a screen monitor, like Hapara Teacher Dashboard, NetSupport or whatever, it is really easy to spot chat happening and stomp on it using your favourite behavioural management technique.

> Bad behaviour is a behavioural issue, not a technology issue.

7 Get your lists organised. It's worth getting your working practices sorted out as early as possible. With cloud-based teaching, this means getting your lists of students grouped up and tagged in user groups as early as possible. There are loads of products and solutions out there to help you manage your classroom, such as gClassFolders, Hapara Teacher Dashboard, Google Classroom and Google Drive folders with shares, email lists, Gmail contact groups and school-wide email groups. Get them organised as soon as you can at the beginning of the year. Then you can

get on with the teaching with maximum speed and minimum time spent looking for and distributing work.

8 This is about teaching, not technology. There are a huge number of products and services out there which look attractive for use in the classroom. A lot of them are heavy on time and light on learning. It's all very well spending a whole bunch of time creating a piece of work using technology, but if it takes three times as long to create as to write an essay, how does that help learning?

I encourage you to use Leighton's Three-Step EdTech Test when assessing a technology for use in the classroom:

i. Could I immediately use this technology in every class, every day, with every student to help them learn better, faster, deeper?

ii. Once the students have learned to use it efficiently, will it achieve Step i?

iii. Try every new technology once anyway (just in case).

9 Stop wandering around the class. You remember how you were taught in teacher training to work the classroom? I'm sorry, but it's not always very efficient and means your students may be off task in the cloud-based classroom. The occasional wander is handy to keep kids on their toes, but you can be much more efficient by working their screens from your desk.

Get a classroom screen monitoring system (iTALC is free for PC-based classrooms, Hapora Interact – formerly known as Hapara Remote Control – is a few pounds per student and there are loads of others). Use them to keep a weather eye on the whole class and keep a look-out for whether they are on chat, email, social media, games

sites and so on. A quick question about whether they are on task will solve the problem very swiftly. Quite often they turn out to be doing something creative and task-relevant when I challenge them – which is great. But it's still fun to keep them on the alert!

10 There is no one-size-fits-all solution. There are a lot of vendors out there. Some of them are claiming to sell a panacea which will solve all the educational problems of the world. They aren't. Google Apps is great for sharing, managing, doing serious work and is brilliantly integrated into the global internet ecosystem, but it has only very recently introduced a basic assessment system. Apple tablets and products look nice and have great cameras, but are tooth-achingly expensive and are woeful for doing truly collaborative work without Google Apps installed, and even then they are not great compared to Chromebooks. Moodle has a proper pedagogical design behind it, is fabulous for hanging on to assessment data, allows the creation of awesome quizzes and deep learning but has a high learning curve. And there are tens of thousands of other products out there with their pros and cons. Ultimately, you will need to keep hacking away with what you can get your hands on: try it, trial it, play with it, take measured risks. And don't give up.

Integrating cloud-based educational technology takes time, courage and imagination, but that does not mean we have to know everything. Our job as educators is not to know how to use every system but to guide our fearless young learners into how to use whatever they find in a purposeful, meaningful and educationally valid way.

> … try it, trial it, play with it, take measured risks. And don't give up.

CREATIVITY

1 To be creative you must think about what students do in their everyday lives that can be transferred into their lessons.

   • What do they enjoy?
   • What do they do often?
   • What are they good at?
   • What can they relate to?

   Use their answers to plan your activities.

2 Don't always assume that if it sounds fun or challenging to you that it will be for your students! Ask your students what they like doing. Being creative is as much about being reflective as it is about being innovative.

3 Use students as resources. Getting them to take ownership and control of the lesson allows them to fully buy into their time, knowing it is them who is determining how they use it.

4 Keep it mixed up but have a routine. Too much creativity can cause confusion for your students. Have a set of activities for revision, for writing, for reading, for comprehension and so on.

5 Creativity in the classroom includes:
   • Teaching aids
   • E-learning
   • Displays
   • Spaces
   • Music
   • Events/seasons
   • Resources
   • Questioning
   • Students
   • You

   Mix up the way you present the lesson, talk and give instructions.

6 Always start your lesson with a creative 'do now activity'. Keep them short and snappy, keep the activities topical and make them relate to current news stories.

7 Ensure creativity isn't only linked to being artistic or being able to

create visually stimulating resources/activities. Being creative is the ability to give every student the opportunity to learn in a less conventional way.

8   Buy into your own ideas! Present them with rigour and enthusiasm! Don't limit any activity because of class size – use all your ideas at once if need be! Don't worry about noise, about mess, about others around you! Live for that very lesson, as if it were the last lesson the students may ever have!

9   Learn from others, but always make it your own. Use the plethora of resources available out there (e.g. http://www. cheneyagilitytoolkit.blogspot. com) but make sure the activities or ideas you use are personalised.

10 This is a little bit of a cliché but think outside the box. Don't be confined by what is usually done or what has been done. Be experimental and be accepting of failure.

ASSEMBLIES

TOM SHERRINGTON
@HEADGURUTEACHER

1 Plan a programme of assemblies well in advance so that people have time to prepare something strong and engaging. Ensure that different individuals lead them so that students hear from multiple voices. Assemblies can be taken by new teachers, senior leaders or student representatives; it's important for all members of the community to feel that they can have a voice in assembly.

2 Create opportunities for vertical groupings to have assemblies together, either whole-school or, if space is limited, in vertical subgroups such as houses. Vertical modelling is extremely powerful in setting aspirations high. If you have vertical groupings, use them for rewarding achievement as well as for ethos reinforcement. It's very helpful for younger students to see older students receive awards and to hear of their successes.

3 Keep assemblies simple by selecting one key idea to explore. The impact of an assembly can be lost if it is overly long or convoluted. Plan for ten minutes as an absolute maximum – something punchy is better than a long presentation. Make sure students and visiting speakers know this too. I find that it works well to end by finishing on a key message, pausing and then saying 'Thank you for listening'. This invites applause which helps you to move on to other matters.

4 Use assemblies to model aspirations through content: big ethical dilemmas, challenging topics such as immigration or homophobia, current affairs issues such as elections in the UK or abroad, riots, strikes, wars, human rights issues, important events such as the death of Nelson Mandela. Or introduce philosophical discussions, key areas of political debate, moral questions about poverty, responsibilities as global citizens and so on. Always pitch these topics high, modelling standards and expectations in a deep way.

5 Involve students in a planned manner. At my school, students deliver key notices about charitable events or house competitions, read match reports, conduct mini-debates, give formal readings and report on major school trips and exchanges. It's important that they rehearse and maintain high standards of public speaking, timing and depth. We invite students to take assemblies on a topic of their choice if they have a burning passion to share something.

> We invite students to take assemblies on a topic of their choice if they have a burning passion to share something.

I've found that it never pays to include all students from a class or group in assemblies at secondary level. It is often painful to listen to as they all say one thing, passing a microphone or stepping forward one by one. For the audience, a few students representing a group can deliver a much better presentation. The assembly should be mainly for the audience, not the presenters.

6 Keep an eye on discipline and the appropriate use of humour. Be prepared to stop an assembly to keep order – all too often people find this awkward and will talk over students who are not listening. Humour needs to be fitting. I've seen assemblies about AIDS and poverty go wrong because the delivery veered into humour and the students began laughing inappropriately. Similarly, avoid stereotypes creeping in. I've seen 'naughty kids' do a well-intentioned assembly on knife

crime, but the result was that it was damaging for them. It would have been better if they had spoken on a positive subject which challenged a stereotype about them, rather than reinforcing one.

7 Use props or images to engage students in thinking. Some of my favourites are included on my blog:

- ■ Straw through potato: http:// headguruteacher.com/2013/12/29/ assembly-idea-can-you-get-a-straw-through-a-potato-what-does-that-tell-you/

- ■ Ripstick: http://headguruteacher. com/2012/09/09/ the-ripstick-analogy-if-you-want-to-suc-ceed-you-need-to-commit/

- ■ Lessons from geese: http://www. slideshare.net/fullscreen/ headguruteacher/geese-14161962/1/

- ■ The Hubble Ultra Deep Field as featured in this post: http:// headguruteacher.com/2013/02/24/ great-lessons-8-awe/

A personal favourite was setting up a huge pendulum swinging from the hall rafters with a massive weight on the end. Students were asked to 'trust in the laws of physics' as the weight swung away and back towards their faces!

> A personal favourite was setting up a huge pendulum swinging from the hall rafters with a massive weight on the end.

8 Use videos that will stimulate discussion or emotional responses. There are so many to choose from. One I've discovered recently is this one about Mitchell, a boy with learning difficulties, who has a magical moment with his basketball team. It's moving and powerful: http://headguruteacher. com/2012/12/29/ kegs-assemblies-ethos-aspirations-spirit/.

I've also played the film *Buddha on the Train*, which is about the power of people to have a positive effect on others: http://www.youtube.com/ watch?v=IQUg75Q_t1c/.

9 Use personal stories as part of the mix. Some of the most affecting assemblies at my school have featured stories of personal bereavement, family members in road accidents, interesting family histories, personal achievements and triumphs over adversity. The content is interesting, but the impact is all the greater because students relate to the fact that someone they know is sharing something personal.

10 Think of assemblies as a key driver of your school ethos. I believe our assemblies are essential for doing this as I describe in this post: http:// headguruteacher. com/2012/12/29/ kegs-assem-blies-ethos-aspira-tions-spirit/. Every element says something about the school ethos: the music, stories, moments of reflection, awards and certificates, even the notices. If your students hear that an Oxbridge preparation workshop, house choir rehearsal, Muslim prayer group or Engineering Mentors' meeting is happening, it tells them something about their school community, even if they are not directly involved.

PRIMARY
PRACTITIONER

STEPH LADBROOKE @LEARNBUZZ

1 What's in a name? At the beginning of the year give children the opportunity to name their class. If you like you can ask them to follow a theme that goes with a topic you'll be studying. For example, when my year group studied the rainforests, my Year 4 pupils could choose any rainforest animal, which led to the Monkey Mandrills, the Mountain Lions and the Bengal Tigers. This year I'm the Year 5 teacher and our theme is water so the pupils chose the Dolphins as their name.

If you want to take it a step further, ask your pupils to choose cryptonyms based on the rainforest (or for us this year, the ocean). Whenever the class go online, instead of using their real names they use their cryptonyms. In this way, our class all know who is posting but

they are safe because no one else has this information. It's also a fun way for children to explore a topic more deeply. Pupils have populated lots of Google class maps using their cryptonyms. Here's an example: https://maps.google.com/maps/ms?vps=2&hl=en&ie=UTF8&oe=UTF8&msa=0&msid=208351685251341664008.0004bdbad960530d479ec&dg=feature/.

2 An invisible pupil. I got this tip from the inspirational Ros Wilson during one of her improving children's writing courses. Just as the title suggests, the idea is to have a pupil in class who is invisible. Your invisible pupil will take on a life all of his (or her) own. Pupils of all primary school ages – and perhaps beyond – love the mystery and imagination involved in this idea and you can develop it in lots of directions. For example, ours took on all the writing

67

'mistakes' in the class, he sat next to children who wanted some company and he got ideas about how to write well from every single child, which was a great confidence boost. Over the years we've had a Marmaduke, a Byron, a Humphrey – more than I can recall, offhand, but all brothers of what we called the 'Allbright' family. They've had time machines that have taken them to the ancient Greek theatre where we've had to help with posting a report so that they can bring back the time machine. Another went to the Mary Rose in Tudor times and we helped him create a soundscape of a Tudor ship using the audio editor Audacity before he could return. The possibilities are endless!

In recent years, each brother of the 'Allbright' family has left us with a rainforest mascot. Among the many we've had are Zingo the Toucan, Humphrey the Tapir and King Kong the Chimpanzee. My pupils give the mascot a name and take him home and on their travels, and then share his diary with the class. Sometimes our mascot goes further afield – Zingo the Toucan made it to the Himalayas with a local authority adviser and blogged throughout his trip! Later that year, he went to the Members' Dining Room at the Houses of Parliament (and received his own security pass!) with a group of the Year 4 Mountain Lions to explain how we'd helped our community to get online!

3 Develop your class as a community of enquiry. Build in opportunities for pupils to explore and develop their thinking skills through enquiries and you'll see why I cannot recommend this highly enough. Based on the ideas behind Philosophy for Children (P4C), enquiries give children opportunities to respond to a range of prompts from a story, newspaper article, artefact, piece of music or picture – anything really – with their own questions and then their own discussion. The prompts can be related to something you're studying or real flights of fancy – you'll be amazed at the quality of discussion and thinking that emerges. If you'd like to take things a step further, Sapere run courses (www.sapere.org.uk) and you might like to check out the Gallions School in East London

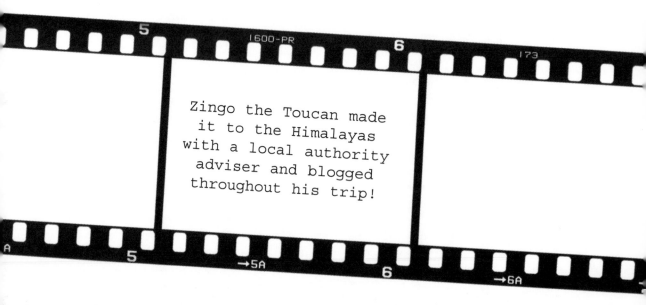

Zingo the Toucan made it to the Himalayas with a local authority adviser and blogged throughout his trip!

which has seen some remarkable outcomes through P4C: www.gallions. newham.sch.uk/index.php?option=com_ content&view=article&id=32&Itemid=14/.

For just a taster of enquiries try Thunks® (www.thunks.co.uk). These are questions to get your pupils thinking like:

'Can a fly see a skyscraper?'

'Can you turn a sound upside down?'

and

'If you could take a pill that meant you'd never fail, would you?'

These will lead to discussions that will surprise, if not amaze, you.

4 VoiceThread. There are many fantastic websites and tools out there but one which I've found invaluable time and again over the last few years is VoiceThread (https:// voicethread.com). Each VoiceThread you create is based on a picture or photo which pupils respond to using a choice of doodle pen, typing, voice recording or camcorder. You can create individual identities for each class member (mine are based on their rainforest or ocean animal cryptonym). We've used them for many things, such as responding to maths questions, contributing information they have found for topics and for evaluating art and D&T projects. There's a free edu version available if you contact VoiceThread using a school email address.

5 Lollipop sticks. Create a named lollipop stick for each member of your class which can then be used in lots of ways. Often they're used when you or the class are asking questions and you don't want to keep choosing the same four or five children who regularly put up their hand. This encourages everyone to think about a possible answer. Avoid anxiety by giving children an opportunity to 'think, pair and share' beforehand, so that they've talked about their answer with someone else, and give them the opportunity to respond to the question with their 'talk partner'. The lollipop sticks are also useful if you want to create pairs or teams or for any activity needing a random element.

6 Movies. Movies feel real in a way that just reading or writing about something really doesn't. Children have used film to make news broadcasts about Hurricane Sandy, the St Jude's Day storm and

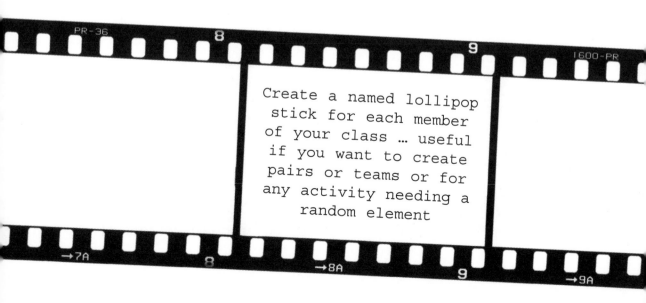

Create a named lollipop stick for each member of your class ... useful if you want to create pairs or teams or for any activity needing a random element

> You really don't need a detailed roadmap for bringing the outside world in, just a willingness to give children opportunities to pursue their interests

the deaths of Henry VIII's wives (in costume!). They've created videos about their Polar Bear Project Action Plans and, most recently, they've filmed their Maths Casts – explaining calculation methods – to post on YouTube. There's just something about a film project that invariably brings together and develops all sorts of skills, from planning, researching, scripting and acting to ICT, working to a tight deadline and collaborating in teams. All you need is something you and/or your pupils can film with. If you have access to iPod Touches or iPads, think about using iMovies which enables pupils to top and tail their films for a professional finishing touch.

7 Class rewards. Here are two ideas for rewards that have proved popular with my pupils. The first one is for tidying the class – something everyone, including children, can feel reluctant about at one time or another! Each table of children works together as a team to tidy their table and the 'peripheral' classroom area (why not squeeze a bit of maths vocab in while we're at it!). The tidiest table wins the cushions which they can sit on throughout the next day of lessons.

Treasure tokens are the other popular reward. Children are given a raffle ticket or treasure token for all sorts of things. Usually it's unexpected and is for being kind and doing something for someone else. The tokens they like best are the ones they give to each other – they write the reason on the back and choose whether they wish to put their own name to it. At the end of each half term, we have a draw and the first person chooses the main activity for an afternoon and the first eight can use the iPod Touches. The first 20 receive a small prize from the treasure token chest (usually pound shop stuff). If someone's name comes out more than twice they give the additional token to a friend in class. Very popular!

8 Real world. My pupils love opportunities to bring the real world into the classroom. This is possible with pretty much anything you're studying in class. Over the years we've had a Black Country history project which involved the children creating a large playground

Pupils in my class think about their learning skills and set themselves targets which they review later in the year.

sculpture of an anchor. The project grew like topsy with children hammering the chain at a chain maker's furnace and arc welding the final structure. They've visited factories, created living histories with their families and learned Old English dialect. We've had a rainforest project which led to pupils campaigning for better labelling of palm oil in products – a major cause of deforestation. My pupils now watch over an area of endangered rainforest in Borneo with the agreement that they'll flag it if they spot any signs of fire or logging (check out Earthwatchers for more information: http://earthwatchers. cloudapp.net). This year my class have created polar bear action teams to try to tackle some of the causes of the loss of Arctic habitat. You really don't need a detailed roadmap for bringing the outside world in, just a willingness to give children opportunities to pursue their interests a bit further afield and encourage them to believe in their ability to make a difference. Small changes can lead to big impacts.

9 Learning skills. Developing good learning skills is at the heart of good learning outcomes. As a school, we've identified the key areas as: independence, curiosity, learning relationships, staying power, changing, meaning making and creativity. Children have come up with their own definition for these (https://docs.google.com/ presentation/d/1m26M6UispsoucK-DU6d6A54PlUi3-2eE1OKDuiCW6Qv8/ present?pli=1&ueb=true#slide=id.p14). Pupils in my class think about their learning skills and set themselves targets which they review later in the year. Children also give their reasons for areas they've identified as strengths and weaknesses, and this is always a valuable perspective for me as their teacher.

10 Class stories. There is absolutely nothing new about this one but it's right up there in my top 10 anyway! Children just *love* sharing a good story and, as primary teachers, we're in a privileged position to ensure that it's part of children's experience in school. We've recently shared ancient Greek myths and legends, stories from George Layton's *The Fib* and, thanks to Axelle, my French-born PGCE student, *Le Petit Prince*, a French children's story by Antoine de Saint-Exupéry, which is also steeped in philosophy.

Never forget what
it's like to teach
a full timetable

JILL BERRY @JILLBERRY102

FOR SLT

1 Never forget what it's like to teach a full timetable with all the attendant pressures. You have different priorities from those who aren't SLT but the majority of them will already be working hard. Your job is to help them to be the best teachers/pastoral staff they can be and not just to keep adding to their load/causing them stress.

2 In your own teaching you have to be credible and be seen to be doing a good job. So practise what you preach and ensure you don't miss deadlines/cut corners/get your priorities wrong. Anything which damages teaching and learning (your own or other people's) has to be avoided at all costs. You don't have to be the best teacher in your department. You certainly shouldn't be the worst.

3 In order to get the best from people they need to see that you see the best in them. Build on the strengths and don't just get hung up on the weaknesses/problems. Work through your middle leaders in particular. Get the right balance of support and

challenge in your relationship with them.

4 Don't get stuck in your office. Get out and about and be a presence for staff and students, especially at breaktimes, lunchtimes and after school. Be sure to support extra-curricular activities and school events – show you know this is an important way of building relationships and contributing to education in its widest sense. It will be another opportunity to show staff that you are aware of and value the work they put in beyond their classrooms.

5 If you're observing others be as constructive and positive as you can. Think of observation as an opportunity to *learn*, not just to *judge*. If you learn something/ can improve your own practice from what you've observed, be sure to share that with the teacher observed, and encourage them to observe and learn from others, including you.

6 Ensure you're a reflective practitioner and keep up to date with all that's happening in the world of education. Twitter and blogs offer a great opportunity to do this. Encourage others to use this channel too, for mutual support and encouragement as well as to learn from those beyond the school.

7 Consider your skill set and how you can continue to build it. What experiences would give you a clearer grasp of the 'big picture'? Closer work with governors? A fuller understanding of the financial management of the school? More involvement in working with the local community? Try to enjoy being out of your comfort zone and learning new skills, and, in this, be a positive model for students and staff.

8 Consider how best you can support your head teacher. This means being honest and open with him/her, even though you should always be professional and keep any disagreements calm and behind closed doors. But if you don't tell your head if they get it wrong, who else will be brave enough to do that? The head *should* value and respect you for it.

9 Sometimes support for the head will involve helping them to feel good about the job they do. Again, if you don't give positive feedback, who will? Your chair of governors *should*, but governing bodies are often a mixed bag!

10 Headship is the *best* job in the school, so if you have the right temperament and can find the school which aligns with your vision/core principles, then go for it!

> **Ensure you're a reflective practitioner** and keep up to date with all that's happening in the world of education.

1 Always try, don't give up.

2 If you can't do your homework, have a go and you will get it, maybe you can work with someone else.

3 If you are scared to be in the school play, do it anyway, it will be fun.

4 When 'the' Ofsted come to school, just ignore them, it's a normal learning day.

5 If your lessons are boring, just join in, it will be interesting in the end.

6 Listen to your teacher, they know lots.

7 Numeracy is tricky, it will get easier.

8 In literacy if you have to write a lot, just keep going, you will get a break at playtime.

9 Be nice at playtime.

10 Check your work before you give it to your teacher.

GOVERNANCE

SLT 1. See your governors as part of the team, not the enemy. An efficient, effective governing body can support a school to make real progress. They are giving up their time to be there, so they want to help make sure every child has a good learning experience. Make use of their skills and experience.

SLT 2. Provide in-house training for governors. They will be able to go on generic training but will then need to know about the school's specific situation and how they can use what they have learned to make a contribution.

SLT 3. Provide information beyond data. Governors need to ask questions about standards and need to have a good understanding of the context for the information they are given. Don't blind them with masses of graphs/ charts. Provide what they need to know in a form laypeople can understand.

SLT 4. Provide opportunities for governors to see learning first hand. They are not experts and therefore will not be making judgements, but the more they understand the workings of the classrooms, the better the job they can do. This will require an agreed protocol with staff for classroom visits. These should have an agreed focus beyond 'a walk around the school' and include a feedback session where that 'other pair of eyes' can share what they saw.

SLT 5. Encourage an atmosphere of shared responsibility between staff and governors. Invite staff to make presentations to governors about their areas of expertise. Full governing body meetings should not be a closed shop where only SLT provide information.

GOVERNORS 1. Understand your role. Undertake some training in roles and responsibilities as soon as possible after taking on the role. Start with an open mind and the approach of a learner.

GOVERNORS 2. Make time. When you become a governor it is important not to see it as just six full governing body meetings a year. There will be committee meetings, but you also need to build in 'head space' - that is, time to read, understand and consider the various papers/documents that you will be sent. If you can't make that commitment, this is not the role for you!

GOVERNORS 3. Ask questions. This is one of the most difficult tasks for new governors but always have 'Why?' and 'So what?' in your mind. Asking these questions will not only provide you with information but also give staff the chance to consider and review what they are presenting.

GOVERNORS 4. Staff governors are there as governors and should play a full part in meetings. You are not there just to balance the numbers, so all the information above applies to you.

GOVERNORS 5. You are not education experts, but you are an integral part of the school team. Be confident, approachable and remember that this all about the children and their learning.

JULIA SKINNER @THEHEADSOFFICE

77

BUILDING POSITIVE RELATIONSHIPS

@ITSMOTHERSWORK

1   Meet children and parents at their home if you can, at least once. This provides more insight than 100 conversations at the start or end of a school day. Lots of primary schools now do a pre-start home visit. Secondary schools can do this too.

2   If a message is truly important, the bottom of a bookbag is no place for it. Every closely printed sheet of white A4 crumpled in the bottom of a bookbag looks the same. Some may never see the light of day till half term. Messages which change or update a previous message are particularly susceptible to disappearing. Texts or emails will often land more accurately.

3   Remember that parents have commitments to their other children too (and schools already know what some of those are). Schools can't avoid calendar clashes entirely, but if secondary end-of-term parent assemblies aren't timetabled against primary ones, both events will get a better turnout. Schools that require parents of children in different year groups to drop one child at a sports centre on the edge of town at *exactly* the same time as dropping another at the

> If a message is truly important, the bottom of a bookbag is no place for it.

school deserve the death stare.

4   Realise that parents in employment may struggle to get time off in working hours. Some will only have the statutory minimum annual leave and will be saving it for school holidays. Some can only get time off with a lot of notice. Some may have their booked leave peremptorily cancelled. Schools can help by giving lots of notice, providing a choice of appointment/event times, avoiding last-minute changes to the schedule and by not implying that parents who can't attend don't care.

5   Parents not in employment don't necessarily have oodles of 'free' time to spare. Parents not working for an employer may be coping with illness or may have other caring responsibilities for younger children, partners or other family members, friends or even animals. If a school can accommodate a toddler sibling or a puppy for an afternoon, it may be possible for that parent to come in and help out, but otherwise it's hard and (again) not a sign that the parents don't care.

6   Families bear financial costs that schools may not always notice. Whether it's providing a pair of 'always

in school' trainers, ingredients for food technology, specialist clothing for an outdoor event, transport to an unusual venue or something for a tombola prize or harvest festival, every family has its financial limit. For big families or multiple-birth siblings these soon add up. Many families won't tell you this – they'll just miss the event or 'forget' the request. If schools can spot this, and quietly assist, it may make all the difference.

7   Schools need to see the family's view of the obstacle course. The three-minute drive from the school gate to the family's front door is a 25-minute walk with a toddler and a buggy. An 8.30 a.m. start time doesn't seem so feasible if your child with additional needs takes 90 minutes to get ready in the morning. What looks like 'support' to the school (an early morning catch-up class) may be an impossible demand on a family. Schools that engage best with parents step into their shoes from time to time (see tip number 1).

8   Remember parents are adults. Some teachers/head teachers have a special 'talking to the children' voice which they don't always switch off when talking with parents. Some parents' reactions to

this are Pavlovian in a variety of unhelpful ways.

9   Honour children's families as they are and not as some people think they ought to be. Use forms which have spaces for Parent 1, Parent 2, Parent 3 and extension space for more, instead of Mother, Father and so on. Make available additional ticket allocations for events. Create celebration cards for grandparents, siblings or significant others. If 'Auntie Joan' is important to a child, find out who she is and why.

10 If you ever leave a message with someone else for a parent, begin with the words, 'Tell X not to worry' (unless you actually want the parent to treat it as a blue light emergency). The only phrase more scary than 'The school called' is 'The police called'.

1. Read lots to give you a better vocabulary and understanding, also if you have to read a book in lesson but have already read it, you can avoid the usual despondency and think, 'Oh, I've already read that and it was actually quite good.'

2. Do all your homework because, while it may be boring, it will help consolidate your knowledge - if you do it properly!

3. Always behave in lessons because you cannot learn if you are unteachable.

4. Have friends that go to different schools, if you can, because then when you meet them you can completely forget about school and it's good to have a break sometimes.

5. Try out different clubs and extra-curricular activities because they will look good on your CV and you might enjoy learning a new sport or skill.

6 Always listen to teachers, family, friends or random strangers - you never know who you might learn something new from.

7 Be a 'joy to teach' so your teachers actually want to help you learn. They can help you outside the classroom too.

8 Concentrate, because half-learned is worse than not-learned - you will have false confidence and will have wasted people's time.

9 Give each teacher and subject a chance, even if you dislike them, because the root of the problem might be you. That history teacher you hate because she always shouts at you? Well, she hates the way you never stop talking!

10 Try your best in everything because that's all anyone can ever ask for.

COMPUTING
ALAN O'DONOHOE @TEKNOTEACHER

1   Join Computing at School
    (http://community.
    computingatschool.org.uk), the
    free community for
    everyone to support
    computing education. Make
    sure that your details are
    up to date, add your
    location and join
    discussions with teachers
    around the UK who are all
    keen to support each
    other.

2   Attend a Computing at
    School hub meeting near
    you. If there isn't a hub
    nearby, start one. It's a
    fantastic opportunity to
    meet others like you as
    well as those who can
    support you. You don't
    need to be an expert to
    host a meeting, just have
    a willingness to talk to
    others and meet them.

3   Teach someone you love how to create a game using Scratch (http://scratch.mit.edu), with a twist. Teaching is the best way to develop expertise at something. Working together with another person to create a modern-day version of Pac-Man, Super Mario or Marble Madness is a creative way to spend time with someone and, at the same time, enable you to imagine some engaging ways of teaching computing and programming.

4   Develop your confidence with text-based programming by reading a free book. Invent Your Own Computer Games with Python (http://inventwithpython.com) leads you through your first experience of programming with Python and not only shows you how to create games with Python, but also helps you understand how they work.

5   Try answering a question with a question (QWAQ) when pupils tell you something is not working or they are confused. Sometimes just getting them to think about what they are asking you is enough to help them spot a solution to their problem. If you answer their question with an answer, all you are teaching them is dependency on you. When they say, 'I can't get it to work', reply with, 'What are you trying to do?', 'Why is that?', 'What have you already tried?'

6   There is a bewildering range of software, apps, gadgets and gizmos to choose from when teaching computing. However, none of them is going to transform your teaching – after all, they are only tools. Go and watch a colleague from another curriculum area teach and try to find one non-technology based idea that you could transfer to your classroom. Tell your colleague what you liked about it, try it, then report back to your colleague. If it didn't work in the way you expected, tell them and see what happens.

7   Provide lots of opportunities for invention and discovery in your teaching to keep children interested, stimulated, educated and entertained. Asking children to complete worksheets that you have spent hours working on is not necessarily the best way to stimulate their interest and provide challenge. By providing them with 'ready-made learning' you are effectively removing the most exciting parts of the lesson. Start a lesson with an abstract image or curious photograph and ask

them to try to guess what the link is to today's lesson.

8 Write and publish a blog post about something that you have tried in a lesson that went either
(a) amazingly well or
(b) appallingly badly. If you write about (a) it will help you feel smug about your achievements when you look at the blog statistics afterwards. However, by blogging about (b) you'll allow other people to help you solve your problems and you'll find they'll make lots of helpful suggestions.

9 Buy a Raspberry Pi computer for a child that you know (either in your family or in your class) and convince them (like Jack returning from market with the magic beans) that this is a far better computing device than an iPad. (You may need to do some research first.) Agree some realistic targets with them, not national curriculum levels but realistic goals - for example, switching it on, creating a game, controlling a robot. When they manage to achieve a goal you've agreed, make such a big fuss that they think you've gone mad!

10 Teach children how to problem solve through stealth by incorporating Sabotage into your lessons. There are lots of different ways to use Sabotage - one is where they agree a list of things that might stop their computer from working. Then they deliberately meddle with their working computer and coach their partner through fixing the faults and restoring the computer. There is another example at http:// teachcomputing.wordpress. com/2013/11/23/ sabotage-teach-debugging-by-stealth/.

CREATING INDEPENDENT LEARNERS

DAVE ANDRESS @PROFDAVEANDRESS

1. Preparing students for university means preparing them for an environment more unlike sixth form than they can probably grasp – without terrifying them!

2. Lecturers aren't judged by how many students do well, but by how well they maintain standards. Students need to be prepared for a completely different kind of relationship with them.

3. Take into account that your students will encounter courses where lecturers aren't interested in hearing lecture material repeated back to them. How can you prepare them for the need to always go beyond what they've already been told?

4. University work is very rarely about finding the 'right answer' – it's about knowing what makes a good answer, and what kind of thought should be behind it.

5. Academic work is about finding a space in an ongoing conversation between experts – which means learning to accept that your sources don't, and won't, agree.

6. Students need to know how to make decisions about reading – when to skim, when to focus, how to take notes when they won't have time to take notes on everything – and that this is a skill that takes practice.

7. Try not to train your students to treat reading like fishing – an exercise in netting a few fat quotations to drop into an essay. Lecturers are not impressed by the ability to copy things out, especially if there is no other sign that the student understands the context or implications of the passage.

8. Students need to embrace the idea that sometimes spending a whole working day getting to grips with a book really is necessary!

9. If you can, try to convince your students that they don't need to take *every* opportunity to party – this is, seriously, the hardest part of the transition for many of them!

10. Lecturers won't force help on students, but they will always be willing to give it if asked. Learning to reach out, having the strength to recognise their own weaknesses, is vital preparation, if you can help your students develop it.

INSPEC

Let's remind ourselves why we are in this business. What do we love about teaching?

Why is our subject important?

TION

MARY MYATT @MARYMYATT

1 We need to know our groups as people first and learners
   second. The headlines are fine - it's not about knowing
   every detail of their life history - but they do need to
   know that we see them as individuals. It's the basis for
   managing behaviour, giving feedback and fine-tuning
   support.

2 Let's remind ourselves why we are in this business. What do
   we love about teaching? Why is our subject important?
   Something happens when we tap into the bigger reasons for
   following our profession. Enthusiasm shines through and
   it's infectious.

89

3   Make the learning explicit by talking about it. This is not the same as stopping every ten minutes to check progress. But it is about asking students to say why they are doing something. Can they make any connections with other subjects or with their lives? What questions do they have? Making time for questions covers lots of bases - it is a great way of unpicking misunderstandings, it deepens motivation and sets the tone that there is serious learning going on here.

4   Let's make sure we are giving honest feedback - comments and questions that move learning on. Marking and feedback should be seen as an ongoing conversation, one where selected pieces of work have comments from the teacher, responses from the student and possibly comments from others in the group. And evidence that thinking has gone further. It is not possible to do it for every piece of work, so don't let's kid ourselves it is. Let's do fewer things, really well.

5   We don't need to put on a show. We aren't in a pantomime. It's exhausting and it can usually be spotted a mile off. It's about raising our game and doing what we know our students need, without cheap tricks. We are free to teach as we think best meets the needs of our students. Sometimes it's lively, collaborative, messy stuff. Sometimes it's silent. And sometimes it's a matter of being at the front, talking. Any of the above are fine, if they are having an impact. Because it's the effect on students' learning that matters, not what techniques we use to get there.

6   Use support. If there's a teaching assistant in the classroom they need to be supporting learning, not photocopying or doing the work for the children. They have to navigate a difficult route through careful questioning and appropriate information so that children make progress. And it's our job to support them. We need to think carefully about how and where we ask our teaching assistants to work. Should it always be out of the classroom? Why?

7   Pay attention to high quality literacy. We need to be very clear about our contribution to children's literacy. So, beyond the technical vocabulary and lists of connectives, what are we doing to *really* bring language alive? Do we encourage play with words? Do we make a point of searching for word roots? Do we give speaking and listening as much

importance as spelling, punctuation and grammar? Do we talk about our own enjoyment of reading?

8   We do need to know the data. And if data isn't your thing, there is someone in school who is paid to make sure you know what it means for your classes. It should not be driving every lesson, but unless we know whether our students are broadly on track, how can we support them, or in some cases prod them up the backside? And while we are at it, we need to know the headlines for the self-evaluation form and school development plan. Note, the headlines, not 100 pages.

9   Things go wrong. That's life. If you are observed during an inspection and it doesn't go as well as you had hoped, remember that it is a very small percentage of the information being gathered to form a judgement on the quality of teaching. Your marking and feedback, attitudes to learning and progress over time all count too. But if you believe you have been unfairly judged, be prepared to complain, via the head in the first instance.

10 Be kind. To yourself, your students and your colleagues. Eat, sleep and smile.

We don't need to put on a show. We aren't in a pantomime. It's exhausting and it can usually be spotted a mile off.

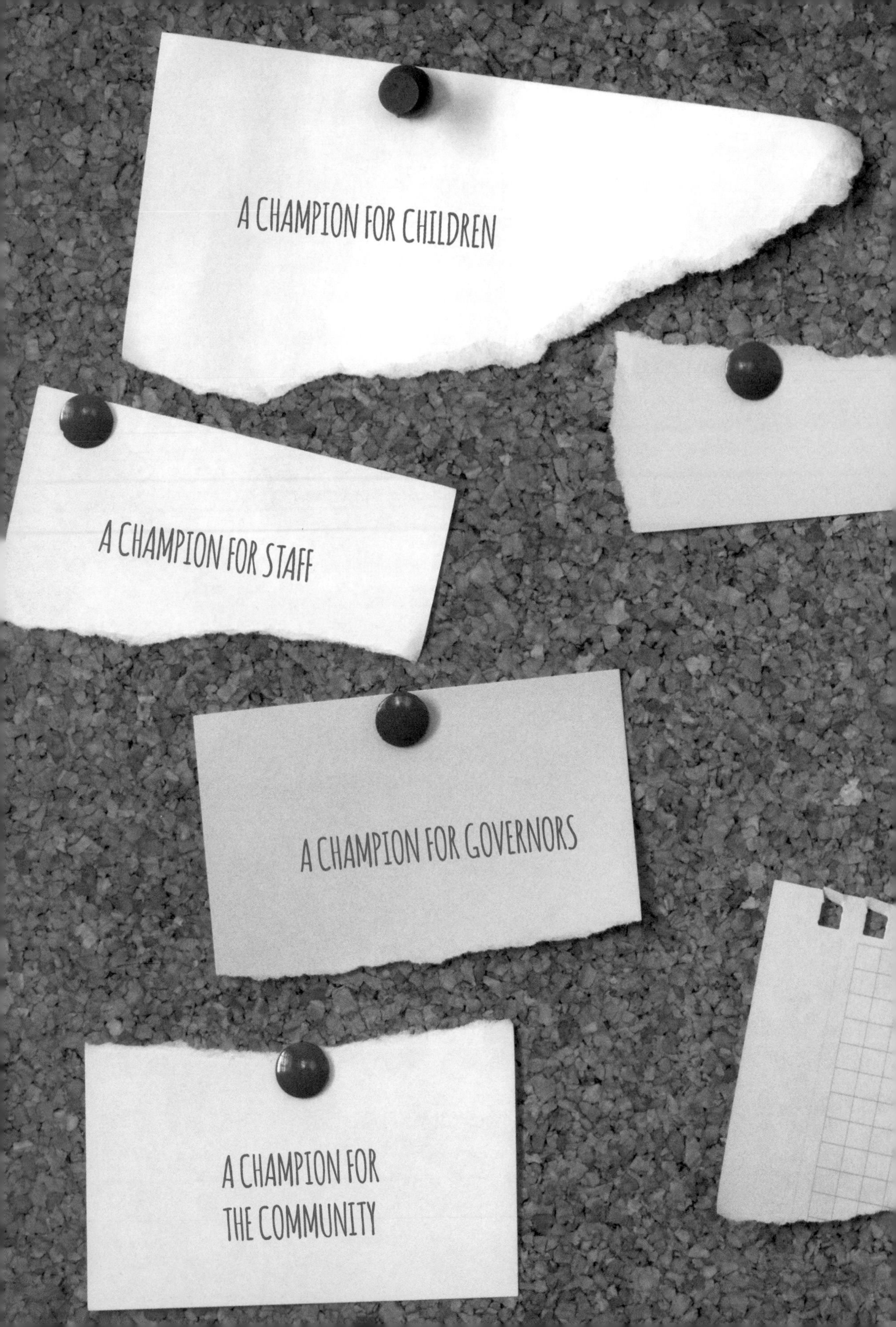

A CHAMPION FOR CHILDREN

A CHAMPION FOR STAFF

A CHAMPION FOR GOVERNORS

A CHAMPION FOR
THE COMMUNITY

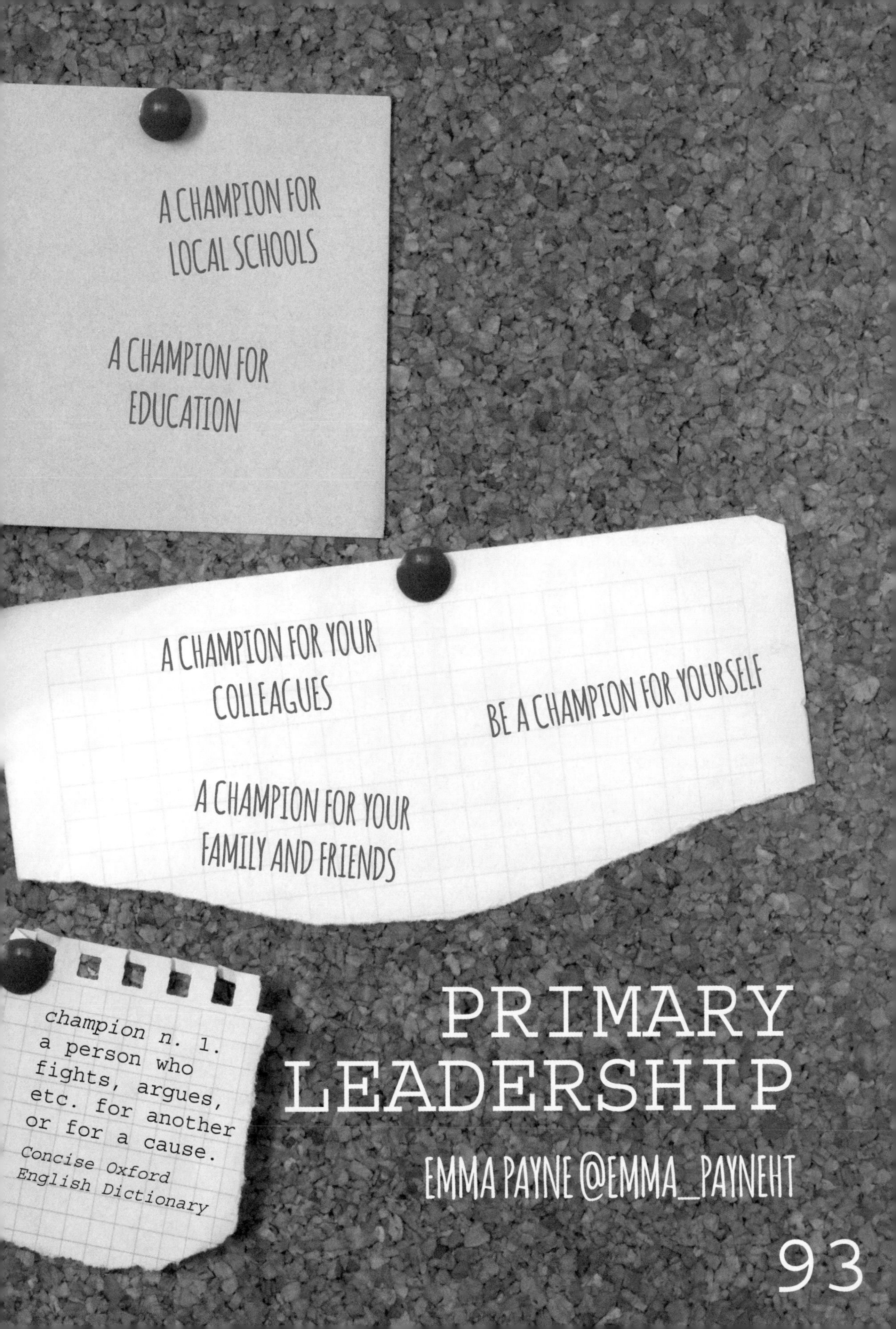

A CHAMPION FOR
LOCAL SCHOOLS

A CHAMPION FOR
EDUCATION

A CHAMPION FOR YOUR
COLLEAGUES

BE A CHAMPION FOR YOURSELF

A CHAMPION FOR YOUR
FAMILY AND FRIENDS

champion n. 1.
a person who
fights, argues,
etc. for another
or for a cause.
Concise Oxford
English Dictionary

PRIMARY
LEADERSHIP

EMMA PAYNE @EMMA_PAYNEHT

93

1 BE A CHAMPION FOR CHILDREN

Put the children at the centre of your decision-making process. 'What is in the best interests of our children?' And if that means you are contravening what the secretary of state says ... then go for it. In the current climate, children are being forgotten in a morass of policies that directly affect them. Defend the children in your school and their right to be happy, safe and well educated. You may be their only protector.

2 BE A CHAMPION FOR STAFF

Treat your staff with respect and trust. Provide excellent professional development that meets their needs. Model what behaviours you want – be the baddie in the staff panto, clean up the sick. Be the gatekeeper – learn to say 'no' as well as 'yes'. Protect their time – no unnecessary meetings and make sure they can attend their own child's nativity play.

3 BE A CHAMPION FOR PARENTS

Be at the gate or entrance daily. Chat to parents, learn their names (and those of their toddlers and dogs!). Be interested and develop relationships; it is amazing what some parents will tell you in an informal setting yet they would never volunteer to come to your office. If a parent needs help to apply for free school meals or a secondary school place, make sure that assistance is provided. If a parent needs advice on parenting skills or housing, be in a position to signpost to other services. Be an advocate for parents.

4 BE A CHAMPION FOR GOVERNORS

Enable governors to challenge you, and the school, effectively by sharing appropriate information, by providing papers on time and by inviting governors into school. Listen and learn from your governors. Support their work by linking with local and national governor organisations.

5 BE A CHAMPION FOR THE COMMUNITY

Use your standing as a head teacher for the good of the community. Challenge authority to listen and respect the needs and opinions of the community – talk to the police, local council, neighbourhood partnerships.

6 BE A CHAMPION FOR LOCAL SCHOOLS

Collectively head teachers have responsibility for all children in all local schools in the local area, so champion *all* children. Don't behave in isolation; think about the impact of what decisions you make will have in other schools. Link and learn together, whether formally or informally, same phase or cross phase.

7 BE A CHAMPION FOR EDUCATION

You are an expert in education, so make your voice heard. If you don't like what the secretary of state is doing to education then tell the world; explain what is wrong, what is right. Be a voice for children, for teachers, for now, for the future. Talk, tweet, blog, write to newspapers, explain to parents, campaign.

8 BE A CHAMPION FOR YOUR COLLEAGUES

Gosh, headship is a lonely job. Support your colleagues with the job, through the tough times, the normal everyday role, and remember to celebrate the successes! Be a shoulder to cry on, an ear to rant at, to provide a cup of tea, a hanky, a pint, a pizza ... Share your stuff: why should we all agonise over the same thing? We can't all be brilliant at everything.

9 BE A CHAMPION FOR YOUR FAMILY AND FRIENDS

They need *you*, not the head teacher part. Forget your work, be yourself. Talk, play, hug. Try not to offload the day's/week's rubbish on to your loved ones – they may have had a worse time than you. Retain your interests – get some more! From politics to reading, baking, cycling, painting, gardening and snowboarding ... Remember, you need something else to talk about!

10 BE A CHAMPION FOR YOURSELF

If you can't champion yourself, how can you champion anyone else? Do the eat healthily thing, the exercise thing, the treat yourself thing. I think the work–life balance thing means work is work but live your life! It's a struggle, but actually to be great at your job you need to be great at being you.

SO LOOK AFTER YOURSELF: YOUR BODY AND YOUR MIND.
BE BRILLIANT, BE A CHAMPION.

Remember that some of the best RE is not in your
students' books but on classroom walls, in
discussions, role plays and many other places.

RE

ANDY LEWIS @ITEACHRE @TALKINGDONKEYRE

1 BREAK STEREOTYPES

Everyone knows the RE of the past – you may well have experienced it yourself. Our students deserve to have some of the best and most engaging teaching available, so that moment of, 'But I don't want to be a vicar/nun', is long forgotten. Even within your school there may be little support for RE, so ensure you are leading on pedagogy, new technology and assessment. It's a fantastic moment when a child goes to another a lesson and tells other staff how great RE is. In some schools, rebranding as Philosophy and Ethics has helped to do this.

2 BE RELEVANT

RE is always in the news, and you need to bring this into the classroom. It's brilliant to have an article photocopied from yesterday's papers to start a conversation. Sometimes you need to change your lesson or rejig the scheme of work due to a local, national or international event. On other occasions, it may not fit into anything you have planned, but often RE is the only forum for open discussion and debate about it. Displays such as 'RE in the News', using online scrapbooks or a blog, can be fantastic stimuli.

3 NETWORK

Get on Twitter and use the #REchatUK and #REteacher hashtags, attend the Culham St Gabriel's RE teachers' weekend, join your Standing Advisory Council on Religious Education (SACRE) or organise an RE TeachMeet. Find other RE teachers and share ideas, challenge one another and collaborate on resources and projects.

4 BE GENUINE

Invite in speakers to talk about their practices, visit places of worship, use the original sacred/source texts and purchase genuine artefacts (they're cheaper too!). Inter-faith dialogue can be a key part of this, and many people will be happy to engage with your students and share their beliefs with them. Ensure teaching is not superficial, theoretical or generalist: never say 'all Muslims' or 'all Christians'.

97

5 USE MULTIMEDIA

Video clips and music can bring lessons alive and provide a source of instant engagement. There are numerous websites beyond YouTube for video clips, including TrueTube, WingClips and BBC News. Music can also be used for reflection and as a time for students to consolidate their thoughts. Using a variety of music when students are working can change the tempo and work rate: experiment with Gregorian chants, Buddhist meditation and Hindu mantras.

6 BE PERSONAL

Students will care what you think and will ask you. Think ahead and prepare an answer without being confessional or forcing indoctrination. – perhaps share a story you feel comfortable with. If you are not prepared to answer a question, work out how you will approach the situation beforehand.

7 ALLOW SPIRITUALITY

This is impossible to define but has meaning for believers and non-believers alike. Time needs to be set aside to appreciate the spiritual nature of any given topic. This may link into the promotion of SMSC (spiritual, moral, social and cultural) development, although it is always important that RE is not the sole provider of this in school!

8 BE OPEN

RE is often the only time that students get to discuss issues that are relevant to them. They are not necessarily distracting you from your planned lesson, and they may well be trying to engage in something that is very important to them. Be ready to have honest and difficult conversations in your classroom. Don't avoid them, embrace and enjoy them.

9 DON'T FEAR

Remember that some of the best RE is not in your students' books but on classroom walls, in discussions, role plays and many other places. You can worry about the lack of evidence of progress in their books, but your students' engagement and enthusiasm for the subject will be clearly evident to any visitor. Encourage them to talk to any guest in your lesson.

10 KEEP YOUR SENSE OF HUMOUR

There are many jokes about religion – many originate from believers about themselves. Often students get confused, but there is nothing wrong with a kind smile. My favourite was when one student genuinely replied to the question, 'Why did Jesus choose 12 disciples?', with, 'So there was one for each month when he made his calendar!'

INCLUSION

CHRIS CHIVERS @CHRISCHIVERS2

Inclusion is, in reality, doing your
job really well for each and every
child for whom you are responsible.

1 Make sure that the school policy for inclusion is written in such a way that it is easily understood by the wider audience, has the potential to impact on the overall school ethos and can be tracked and evaluated regularly. Reference is likely to be made to associated policies, such as behaviour, safeguarding, parents and teaching and learning (all abilities).

2 Interpret the broader policy into a shortened series of memorable statements. Translate as needed for any significant heritage groups. Display expectations clearly around the school and refer to them regularly in class or in assemblies.

3 Clear lines of responsibility are essential. Good record keeping at all stages is a hallmark of effective, supportive practice. Record keeping should be streamlined but be easy for staff, parents and external experts to effect, and be seen to have impact in supporting the school's ability to support the children.

4 Communication, in all its forms, is the bedrock of successful inclusion between all parties. Easy access for parents to key teaching staff can limit the impact of potential issues. Reduce the time for parents to brood on a possible problem. Parents can be the answer to successful inclusion; it is essential that children see the school and parents working together with a common purpose.

5 Know your children really well, particularly the identified vulnerable ones, but also know what to look out for so that no one slips through the net. Know their personal situations as well as their academic achievements. Ensure that this information is known by those with a need to know – classroom teachers as well as mentor staff.

6 Plan for individual personal support. Allocate a specific member of staff to be the front-line mentor and support. Where there are a number of vulnerable children, ensure that each mentor has a manageable number to monitor.

7 Teachers should differentiate appropriately in academic situations. This can take a variety of forms but should provide challenge, as well as opportunities to succeed, to all abilities. Descriptions of different differentiation approaches are described in this article: http://www.inclusionmark.co.uk/index.php/learningteaching/learning-and-teaching-ideas/analyse/differentiating-differentiation/.

8 Ensure teachers' responses to children's needs are personalised in learning situations.

This can be seen in:

- Inputs which allow for a breadth of ability through careful vocabulary selection, use of appropriate resources, use of metaphor or reference to prior learning.

- Questioning quality, initial and scaffolded subsidiary questions.

- Oral feedback within the lesson which should provide support and guidance to the next learning steps.

- Marking which adds value to subsequent learning and which is enacted quickly to have impact.

9 Evaluate and reflect on the system regularly, from individual examples to corporate level, to quality assure the whole system, seeking and utilising feedback from everyone concerned. Inclusion is embedded in the *Teachers' Standards*.[1]

10 Inclusion is, in reality, doing your job really well for each and every child for whom you are responsible. It is the teacher's role to find the best way to help a learner to learn. Learners are learning to become learners; they are on a long journey to becoming experts.

---

1   Department for Education, *Teachers' Standards: Guidance for School Leaders, School Staff and Governing Bodies* (2011, updated June 2013). Ref: DFE-00066-2011. Available at: https://www.gov.uk/government/publications/teachers-standards.

EDU READS

CROWD SOURCED BY JON TAIT @TEAMTAIT

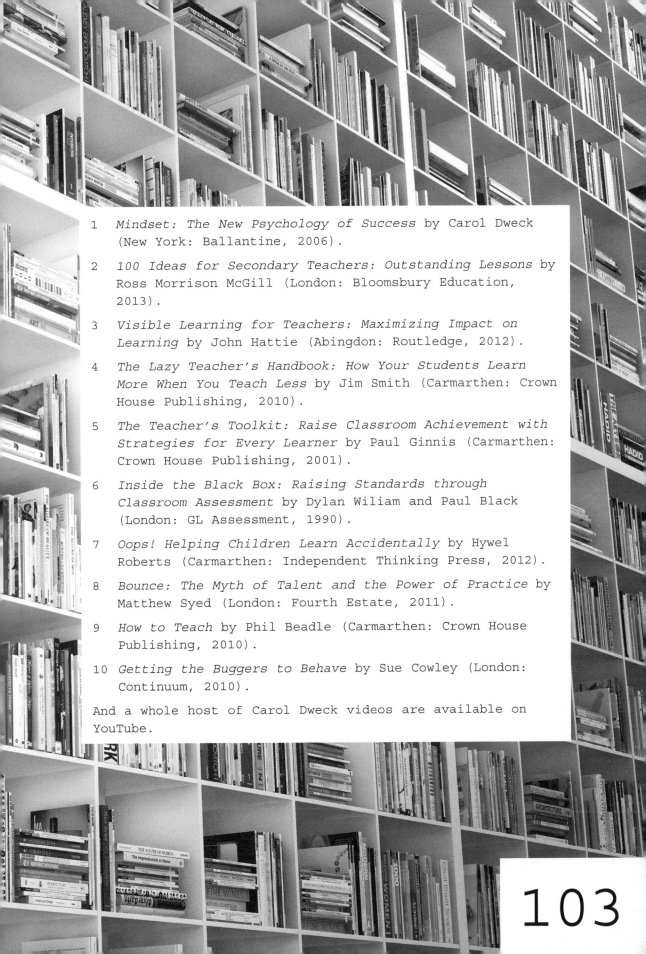

1 *Mindset: The New Psychology of Success* by Carol Dweck (New York: Ballantine, 2006).

2 *100 Ideas for Secondary Teachers: Outstanding Lessons* by Ross Morrison McGill (London: Bloomsbury Education, 2013).

3 *Visible Learning for Teachers: Maximizing Impact on Learning* by John Hattie (Abingdon: Routledge, 2012).

4 *The Lazy Teacher's Handbook: How Your Students Learn More When You Teach Less* by Jim Smith (Carmarthen: Crown House Publishing, 2010).

5 *The Teacher's Toolkit: Raise Classroom Achievement with Strategies for Every Learner* by Paul Ginnis (Carmarthen: Crown House Publishing, 2001).

6 *Inside the Black Box: Raising Standards through Classroom Assessment* by Dylan Wiliam and Paul Black (London: GL Assessment, 1990).

7 *Oops! Helping Children Learn Accidentally* by Hywel Roberts (Carmarthen: Independent Thinking Press, 2012).

8 *Bounce: The Myth of Talent and the Power of Practice* by Matthew Syed (London: Fourth Estate, 2011).

9 *How to Teach* by Phil Beadle (Carmarthen: Crown House Publishing, 2010).

10 *Getting the Buggers to Behave* by Sue Cowley (London: Continuum, 2010).

And a whole host of Carol Dweck videos are available on YouTube.

1. Keep organised. Have all work organised using folders, dividers and headings so it is easier to access.

2. Revise as you go along. Revising throughout the year means materials are ready and much has already been learned, making it easier to remember.

3. Keep on top of your work. Don't put off pieces of work - they need to be done sooner or later. The longer you leave it, the more it builds up.

4. Practice makes perfect. Make sure your notes are up to scratch and that practice work or homework is good. The more it is done, the more likely it is to be perfected.

5. Address issues early. Anything you don't understand, or if there are problems getting in the way of your learning, solve them early to stop them from being prolonged.

6. Listen to others. Distracting others or allowing yourself to be distracted can mean you or someone else may miss important pieces of information from a teacher or student.

7. Have all the notes. Make sure you have all the notes in plenty of detail. If not, get them from a presentation, peer or textbook then copy into your own words so you understand it.

POST 16, YEAR 13 PUPIL

AMY KENNETT @AMYKENNETT

8 Manage your time. Manage time between work and fun. Too much work can lead to failure, but too much fun can lead to failure also. Find a balance and work on building up that balance early.

9 Revise. Revision is the only way to learn. Start early so there's not an end-of-term rush to learn things. Starting early also means you can try out different things and see what works for you.

10 Enjoy your learning. There's nothing better than knowing you've done the best you can do, so take pride in your work. Knowledge is unbuyable. The greatest gift a person can receive is the gift of knowledge, so be proud to be learning.

HALF THE
SCARY FUN

IAN GILBERT @THATIANGILBERT

1 **Think for yourself**. By all means ask around, borrow ideas, read and listen, Tweet and blog, but when it's you and the learners, remember, it's just you and the learners. It's not just OK to think for yourself and make it up as you go along, it's half the scary fun. If anyone asks, tell them you are taking an emergent approach drawn from complexity theory and have they read any of the work by Davis and Sumara?

2 **Don't think for them**. 'Don't ride the bike for them' was a great piece of advice I received a long time ago. Struggling, stuttering, feeling stupid and staring silently into space for long periods are all signs that thinking is taking place. Let the child get on with it. For themselves. If you finish their sentence or complete the task for them the message they get is, 'I'll take it from here'. If you want proof, watch Dara Ó Briain's *School of Hard Sums*. You get to watch someone who is good at maths do maths easily. It won't help you do maths though.

'Don't ride the bike for them'

3 **Thinking hurts more than learning**. I oscillate between considering thinking a subset of learning and learning a subset of thinking. Whichever it is, they are linked but not the same thing. My experience tells me children spend more time learning at school, something that may not involve a great deal of thinking, than thinking, which may not involve any obvious learning. A useful rule of thumb, however, is if they complain that their brains hurt then they have probably been thinking rather than learning.

4 **You are not and never should be a facilitator**. There are some who are against this word because it is the opposite of what they see the teacher's role should be, that of the subject expert at the head of rows of subdued children who are passively absorbing the best of what is known conveyed through the medium of the teacher's golden prose. My personal issue

with the word is not that. It is the fact that the word literally means to 'make easy' and therefore implies easy is a good thing. It's not. Rewardingly hard is a good thing.

5 **Never assume**. We don't know what thinking looks like. Or learning. A child sitting in an Ofsted-friendly pose, all bright-eyed and pen poised, may give the impression of being ready for learning but that may be the point. If I look like I'm learning then the teacher may not ask me any of those awkward questions to check whether I am or not. And that child slumped, tapping his pen and staring into space? Remember, you genuinely have no idea what's going on in there. How do you look when you're thinking? Or learning?

6 **Use your data to improve your children**. Not the other way round. You can't construct a child out of test scores. They are living, breathing, mewling, puking things with a right to be treated as an individual and not a piece of data. The problem is that when education becomes a market (as is happening globally) that market demands data. Hence the focus on baseline tests, high-stakes tests, tests for three-year-olds, PISA tests, performance-related pay, league tables, inspection results and everything else that turns people into scores. Use the data by all means, but in the children's interests not yours.

7 **VAK is a tool in the way that a drill isn't a hole**. Each year, it seems that this year's bandwagon seems to be pointing and laughing at people on last year's bandwagon. Six Thinking Hats. Bloom's taxonomy. Circle time. SOLO taxonomy. Multiple intelligence theory. They're all just tools. A way of making things happen. Good things usually. Structured thinking. Deeper thinking. Wider thinking. Better thinking. Engaging learning. Deeper learning. Learning that doesn't just bounce off but actually sticks. It's all about variety really. We're different and so different

> You can't construct a child out of test scores.

things work at different times, especially when it comes to helping children get themselves unstuck. Some in this book will disagree with me on this, but they're as wrong as they think I am.

8 **Don't close the door on the world when you close the door to your classroom.** You might be a subject teacher but you are much more than that, if you want to be. In my languages classroom I had a panel that I used for Amnesty International posters. I didn't make a big thing of it but I made a thing of it. I used to play world music when the classes were coming in. They didn't like it but they weren't supposed to. I had odd posters up at various times. I set them a quiz with questions like, 'If the French for weekend is "le weekend" and the French for hamburger is "le hamburger", what's the French for combine harvester?' I wanted them to learn about life, death, struggle, humour, music, poetry and art as well as French. Probably more so if I'm honest.

9 **All that Twitters is not gold.** There are some eloquent, strident, plausible educational voices on the internet today, people who are unemployable in a school setting. Don't be bullied into thinking that there is only one way of doing something and that is their way. My advice is the louder someone insists they're right, the more they should be ignored. In fact, when you meet a clever person telling you

> … when you meet a clever person telling you this is how it is, go and find someone cleverer.

this is how it is, go and find someone cleverer. And make sure you seek out those great practitioners who are just getting on and doing the job well, with their mind like a parachute, all stretched out and dishevelled by the end of the day.

10 **Don't always do things in tens.**

TEN PRE-TEACHING THINKING POINTS FOR LITERACY

MARTIN ILLINGWORTH @MARTINILLINGWOR

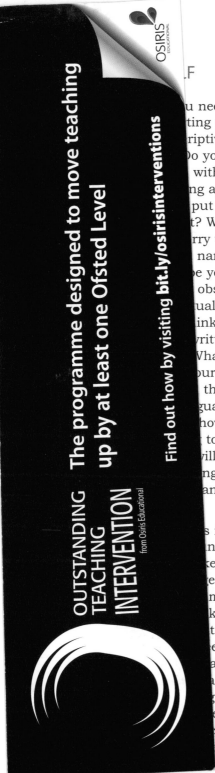

...LF

...u need to look at
...ting point might
...riptivist who is a
...Do you carry a
...with you looking
...ng apostrophes?
...put up with a
...t? While out
...rry where the
...name
...e you are a
...observe the
...ually use
...ink change is
...ritten grammar
...What will your
...ur students?
...they form of
...guage based on
...how language
...to suggest that
...ill you accept
...nge, especially
...anguage is so

...s in your
...nding
...e a look at the
...e 2 spelling,
...mar test. Even
...k at the
...t Key Stage 3
...ed to brush
...are you in
...age? Look
...uistic
...evel language
...ted to deal
...emantics,
...ragmatics.
Inform yourself about these terms.
Are you confident when approaching
audience, purpose and context – the
keys to language production and
reception?

KNOW YOUR STUDENTS

3 What skills do your students
already have that you can tap
into? Could you audit the qualities
of the students' writing and make a
hit list of common needs and also
focus on individual needs? Look
across the genres of writing and
speech. Where are the confidences
and where is the hesitation from
your students? What are the literacy
practices that are distinctive to your
subject? What are the literacy
practices that you want students to
remember as they travel across the
curriculum? Your students, the
digital natives, will already be adept
at creating new language approaches
when they communicate over the
internet and when using their
mobile phones. This is a new set of
language practices that has no set of
rules and that is highly creative.
Can you tap into this new-found
ability to cross styles and genres?
Can you balance the needs of formal
standard writing for the short-term
goal of an exam with the real-world
need to be able to communicate in
the digital world?

4 What do your students need to
know? This is a broader
question than just preparing them
for examinations and tests. Think
through what it might mean to be
literate in the 21st century. If you
are preparing students to be
functioning and articulate adults in
ten years' time, what will that mean?
Do you expect the adult world of
work to be relying on paper and
pen? Or will there be a whole range
of ways of speaking and writing in
professional and social domains?
(Are the last two sentences
sentences or should they be one?
And does it matter?)

STARTING POINTS

5 Investigating how language is used in the real world strikes me as the way to engage your students in meaningful ways. Lots of the terms of language study are really unlovable and very hard to remember! Can you interest your students in how language is functioning and then lead them to an understanding of terminology? How about watching videos of small children speaking and then examining transcripts to see how they learn the structures of the language? No one teaches two- and three-year-olds grammar but they are able to process patterns and apply rules to the words that they hear around them. A research project might get your students thinking about how language works. How about making recordings of students talking to each other and seeing how they use language to tell stories?

6 Mistakes are cool! Mistakes are helpful! Why do we have this preoccupation with students being right first time, every time? Will adult life be like this? Do we get our best ideas by following what is already known? Perhaps you could get students to spot mistakes in their own work, in the work of others and in the world around them.

7 Let's change how students feel about their technical skills. Why does a student say, 'I can't spell', when they get four words wrong on a page of two hundred words that they have written? 196/200 seems pretty good to me! Present the journey towards articulacy as a never-ending journey. Move from the functional to the fluent.

APPROACHES

8 Best learning comes when we are collaborating. Best learning comes when we are teaching each other. Best learning comes when we experiment. Best learning is pursuing new knowledge not writing down old knowledge. Best learning comes when we work things out for ourselves. Best learning comes when we see the relevance of the study. Best learning comes when we try things out.

HAVING FUN

9 Get your students to collect funny signs that they see as they go about their lives. Funny signs are everywhere. What better homework could there be? If students are looking out for funny signs, in the process they will be truly examining the world around them.

10 CAUTION: The fun is going out of English lessons everywhere. For that matter, the English is going out of English lessons everywhere! Make room for the aesthetic moment. Make your lessons important for that moment right there and then in the classroom. Let's take our students past functional skills to the joy of the arts. I promise you that if you engage your students with interesting texts and approaches, they will be able to do the exams in the short term and they will leave school prepared for that unknowable future. Give it go!

You tell me what the final ingredient is for the students in your class ...

GEOGRAPHY

DAVID ROGERS @DAVIDEROGERS

1 Need some Ordnance Survey mapping for a location in the UK? Bing and the Ordnance Survey teamed up a while ago and, as a result, you're able to view 1:50,000 and 1:25,000 OS mapping on screen. Great for case studies at GCSE and developing map skills. Simply visit Bing maps (www.bing.com/maps), select 'Ordnance Survey Map' and zoom to the appropriate level. This is like porn for geography teachers!

2 Do you always start off your lesson in English? Ever thought you'd like to mix it up? Imagine your class walking into the room to a starter in Polish or Welsh. There are many free online translation sites out there including Bing Translator (www.bing.com/translator) and Google Translate (http://translate.google.com).

Students will need to collaborate to translate the learning using their own devices.

Read this post by Priory geography member, Sam Atkins (@SamGeoAtkins), where the idea is taken one step further into a whole lesson: http://daviderogers. blogspot.co.uk/2012/06/ guest-post-mobile-priorygeogra-phy-and.html/.

3   Want to improve literacy and the use of geographical terms? Then consider banning certain words in all year groups. For example, ban children using 'stuff', 'things', 'it', 'up', 'left' and so on. This simple idea challenges young people to use the correct terminology. See here for more information: http:// daviderogers.blogspot.co. uk/2006/12/banned-word-board. html/.

4   Got some mobile devices? Use the school grounds and Fotobabble (www.fotobabble. com) to create descriptions of prevailing weather conditions and forecasts. Working in pairs, children have to carefully think about their script in order to communicate effectively. See some examples at: www.fotobabble. com/m/UjlYSDlrT0FQUkU9 and www. fotobabble.com/m/ SThZeWJJcOJQNU09/.

5   Start lessons with the Bing homepage (www.bing.com). The daily image is interactive and high quality. They are also nearly always geographical and link to many topics. For example, challenge the class to identify as many different types of job linked to the image. Does the image show a landscape developed by weather or climate? How many geographical enquiry questions can be developed from the image? As the image is interactive, you can find out where it is as well as key facts.

6   If you haven't used Gapminder World in your lessons yet, do so now (www.gapminder.org). There is a range of teaching tips and lessons attached to the site. I use it wherever there is a development or stats-related issue which, to be honest, is most of geography!

7   Start geography lessons by watching *Newsround* (www.bbc. co.uk/newsround). How many geography news stories are there? What links into what you're studying at the moment? Remember that geography is a dynamic subject, linked to the world outside now.

8   GCSE revision? Get
     revision gamed up with
     this idea from Jo Debens:
     http://www.slideshare.net/
     geogrocks/
     jo-debens-revi-
     sion-games-23610641/.

9   Have a go at banning
     things in lessons. For
     example, combine
     Mission:Explore missions
     with banning pens, pencils
     and paper (see http://
     daviderogers.blogspot.co.
     uk/2010/06/what-happens-when-you-
     ban-pens-pencils.html and www.
     missionexplore.net). Remember
     to give lessons a
     geographical context and
     knowledge base for this to
     be effective, such as
     habitat mapping or map
     skills. Why
     not have
     a go

at banning an entire
country? Can children
prove that a country does
or does not exist (see
http://daviderogers.blogspot.co.
uk/2012/10/simple-but-effec-
tive-ideas-iceland-does.html)?

10   Are you in a geography
     department that hasn't had
     a go at geocaching yet?
     Get on it (see http://
     daviderogers.blogspot.co.
     uk/2011/04/geocaching-what-why-
     how.html)!

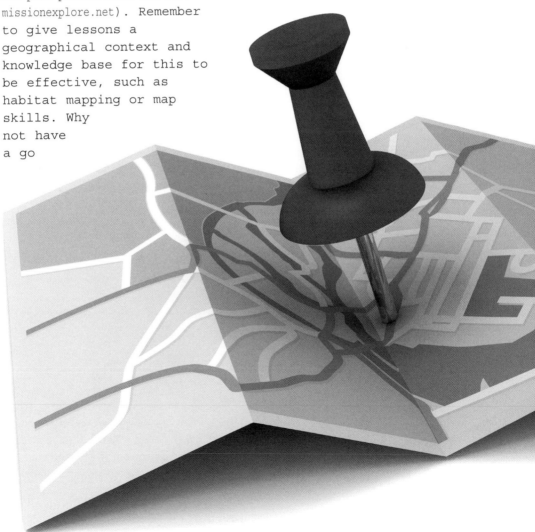

HEAVY METAL LEADERSHIP

117

1 MASTER OF PUPPETS. METALLICA

http://youtu.be/2f1Ny74_ou0

So you're the leader. But are you really in charge? What, really, is the driving force? Who is the real puppeteer, moving everyone around, pulling the strings? Metallica sing about how things get confused, switched around, and what you thought you were controlling is now controlling you. You may think the pupils are at the heart of your school and you are controlling and managing all the other, external, negative influences. But are you? Or are aspirational targets controlling what you say? Or league tables killing you? Or are you really obeying Ofsted like it's your 'master master'? Yes, these will influence how you run the school and you are accountable to them. But should they define you? Do they blind you from your real vision? Shouldn't your passion for education and the pupils in your school ultimately be your motive? Your puppeteer? As leader, you need to ensure that you hold firm to your values. They should control you. And with them you can help shape the best education for all pupils in your school.

2 BEFORE I FORGET. SLIPKNOT

http://youtu.be/v_09wFxoaeQ

'I am a world before I am a man.' Who comes first in your school? You? Your senior leadership team? Your teachers? And even then, upper-pay range teachers? More experienced teachers? NQTs? Teaching assistants? Admin assistants? Kitchen staff? Caretakers? The pupils? There can be hundreds, if not thousands, of people in your school other than you. Every single one of them looks to you. Never forget that. You are a world before you are a man.

3 STARGAZER. RAINBOW

http://youtu.be/UgdSarGbE0g

Are you the wizard? Do your staff feel trapped? Like they are building your stone tower? For you to get your glory? Think carefully about that. Are your staff really empowered? Who do they feel they are working for? Are they trying to be the best they can? If so, for whom? And if not, why not? If staff are working for you, because you've told them to or directed them to, then that's not good enough. It won't impact learning in a meaningful way. And it says a lot about what is core to your school. Everyone should be building that tower together. Including you. You should be the first one to pick up a stone and show people what to do. Show them you care. That you want to help them. And the pupils should also be helping. They need to be integral to their own education. When the tower is built, the feeling of hope should belong to everyone. Never just you.

PLEASE NOTE SOME VIDEOS CONTAIN SWEARING

4   SPIDERS. SYSTEM OF A DOWN

http://youtu.be/SqZNMvIEHhs

The message in this haunting song is control. Watching. Monitoring. How much do you control what goes on in your school? Do you monitor? You probably should do. What do you monitor? Teaching? Or learning? Attainment? Or progress? But perhaps the most important question is why do you monitor? What impact does it have? Who does it help? Accountability and judgement is all very well, but if nothing improves, or there is no intention to support and develop, then perhaps you are just controlling. And is that really OK?

5   EVOLUTION. KORN

http://youtu.be/m8fm3Z7jgWM

Evolution. A process in which something passes by degrees to a different stage, especially a more advanced stage. How does your school evolve? How do you, as a senior leader, ensure evolution occurs? No school should stand still. Your pupils deserve more than that. They deserve constant evolution towards a better state. A better education. Is it about refining what you already do? Or is it about changing things? Trying new things? Innovating? Creating? What if you are already outstanding? Do you need to evolve? But what would happen if you didn't evolve? Evolution is about reaching a higher state. It requires aspirations. Surely we owe our students nothing less.

6   SCHISM. TOOL

http://youtu.be/UhjG47gtMCo

This song is famous for uncommon time signatures and 47 changes of metre. That's a lot of changes to the rhythm. As a senior leader you need to hold the rhythm for your school. It is you that sounds out the heartbeat for everyone else to follow. They can be creative. They can bend the rules. But they need your reassuring steady beat behind them. Tool serve to remind us that this rhythm may not always be straightforward. There will be changes. There will be tricky time signatures to contend with. But just as a heavy metal song would be incomplete without its drummer delivering the forceful, driving rhythm, so our schools would begin to fragment and fail without us sounding this daily heavy metal heartbeat for them.

7   UNDER AND OVER IT. FIVE FINGER DEATH PUNCH

http://youtu.be/ZLk75fFXqH4

You take the fame. What did you hold dear as a teacher? Is it still the same as you do as a senior leader? Should it be the same? As you progress through your career, the way you view your pupils, your school and the education system will undoubtedly change as your responsibilities and accountabilities also change. But should this change you? Should your values change? Perhaps, as a teacher, you didn't give your values too much thought. Should this be something, as leaders, we should encourage our staff to do? As senior leaders, we all embark on our first headship with a clear idea of our values. Indeed, we are often quizzed on them at interview. But do they change as we develop and grow within our role? And do we allow them to change? Or watch as this happens? Fame and success or sanity?

8   DRAG THE WATERS. PANTERA

http://youtu.be/4hx8TW6sYys

'In everyday life, there is more than meets the eye. To reach the depths of truth, we must drag the waters.' Teachers. Parents. Governors. Councillors. The list is endless. What are their motives? What do they want from you? What do they want you to do? As a senior leader you will never know this. And you will never fully understand this. The water is deep. In some places it is fast flowing. In others rather stagnant. It is your job to try to learn what you can. And deal with each person as an individual. But consider, are their motives relevant? Would they change your answer? Should they change your answer? How would you respond? How would you act? There will always be hidden depths to people.

9   ICH WILL. RAMMSTEIN

http://youtu.be/iY-2G4OblWE

Not in English. But it roughly translates to 'I want'. I want you to trust me. I want you to believe me. As leaders we are constantly, and acutely, aware of our wider community and other stakeholders within our school. It is our responsibility to understand them. To help them to understand us. And to work together in the best interests of the pupils. One section of the song cries, 'Can you hear me? We hear you. Can you see me? We see you. Can you feel me? We feel you. I don't understand you.' Those in the community don't always come forward. Many don't want to be reached. What are you going to do about it? Are you going to sit and watch? Are you going to moan about how no one responds? No one cares? Or are you going to get out there? Reach out your hand. Show them. Show them what you do. What your pupils do. Why it matters. It's your responsibility.

10   WELCOME TO THE JUNGLE. GUNS N' ROSES

http://youtu.be/o1tj2zJ2Wvg

So you're thinking of being a senior leader? It's amazing. It's rewarding. It's everything you want it to be. But it will bring you to your knees. Are you ready to enjoy? Are you ready to explore? Are you ready to fight? Welcome to the Jungle.

LAZY TEACHING

JIM SMITH @THELAZYTEACHER

1. Look, listen and learn from others – there is so much talent in the profession.

2. Invite others to learn from you – the sum total of the profession will only improve when you add your new ideas.

3. Involve the students – they have much to offer.

4. Tell the students – they have much to learn.

5. Marking – too much of it and you feel resentful.

6. Marking – too little and they resent you.

7. Value questions as much as answers – it might show they have been thinking.

8. But value their answers with a question – it shows you have been thinking.

9. Book in sleep not lesson planning for the first Monday night of any term – you will be exhausted.

10. Book in lesson planning not sleep for the first Monday night of any term – you will hopefully be buzzing again for the term ahead!

BEING A CONNECTED EDUCATOR

1. Join Twitter and read this blog post on how to make the most of Twitter as a teacher: http://ictevangelist.com/twitter-tweetdeck-lists-hashtags-and-ukedchat/.

2. Read the blog posts on the following link which reflect on 13 highs from 2013 and 14 wishes for 2014: http://storify.com/ICTEvangelist/nurture-13-14/. Then, follow the authors and their blogs on Twitter.

3. Get yourself a smartphone and realise that CPD happens 24/7/365 these days. The days of waiting for CPD to come to you are gone. Make it come to you on Twitter. The hashtags and info on this handy infographic by @TeamTait should help get you started: http://www.edutait.co.uk/2012/04/23/infographics-the-power-of-twitter/.

4. Get yourself to a TeachMeet. You can read more about TeachMeets here: http://ictevangelist.com/what-makes-a-teachmeet-tick/. But if you're looking for one in your local area, visit the TeachMeet wiki and find one local to you and sign up: http://teachmeet.pbworks.com/w/page/19975349/FrontPage/.

5. Get on Pinterest. It's not just a place where you can find recipes. It's a treasure trove of great ideas on teaching and learning. Why not start by having a look at Rachel Jones' great pin boards here: http://www.pinterest.com/rlj1981/.

6. Use Google searches effectively with these ideas: http://ictevangelist.com/ use-google-search-like-a-rock-star/.

7. Why not share some of your amazing findings with your colleagues? A free tool, like Smore, is a great way to share teaching and learning nuggets with your colleagues, such as these: https://www.smore.com/u/ sarahsafraz/.

8. Learn how to use Google Docs (it's called Google Drive now if you can't find it). Simply sign up to Google and access some brilliant collaborative tools for free. Google also own YouTube, in case you didn't know, and so with one single sign on you have access to some brilliant creation and collaboration tools.

9. Get blogging yourself. WordPress. Edublog. Kidblog. Blogspot. Blogger. These are all free tools that you can use to start sharing your practice and reflecting on your work. Why not give it a go?

10. Find time to put your phone down, step away from your computer, put away the marking and get away from it all. The urge to stay connected 24/7/365 is huge, especially in the high stakes arena of education. Make sure you find time for yourself. The world won't end if you don't keep up with your timeline.

MARK ANDERSON @ICTEVANGELIST

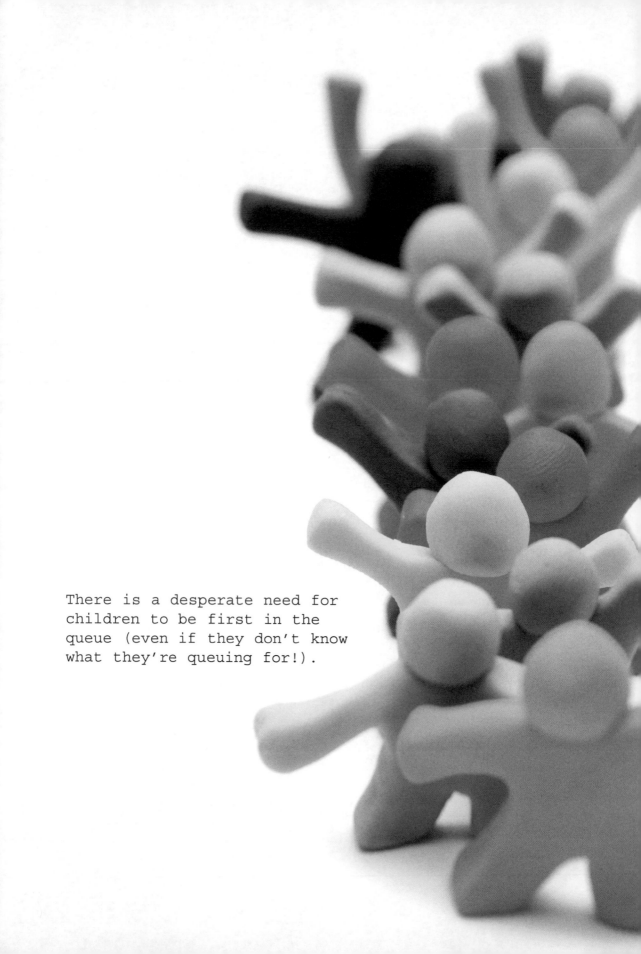

There is a desperate need for
children to be first in the
queue (even if they don't know
what they're queuing for!).

SURVIVING YEAR 3

(ESPECIALLY AFTER SEVERAL YEARS IN YEAR 6)

BEN WALDRAM @MRWALDRAM

1 EXPECTATIONS

Year 3 can, and will, achieve far more and far higher than you think. If you set the bar high, they will aspire to reach it. Algebra and semicolons in Year 3? Doable. Have high expectations of what they *can* do, but readjust your expectations of what they *will* do.

2 PARENTS

Parental engagement is key. In upper school (and beyond) I rarely got to see parents; in Year 3 I do every day. Chatting to them about the positive and negative aspects of their child's day, touching base about homework, friendships, playtimes and more is hugely important. I put a lot of effort into this as it pays dividends. Don't be miserly with your precious time – speak to these parents.

3 LINES

There is a desperate need for children to be first in the queue (even if they don't know what they're queuing for!). Lines are often more of a squiggle too. I get them to raise their hands above their heads to create a 'target' which I then 'fire an arrow' through. Simple but effective. As for 'Who's first in the line?', this is always dependent on who is lining up best in the line –

they get promoted to the front. Nothing revolutionary, but it works well.

4 TOILETS (PART 1)

If a Year 3 asks to go to the toilet, let them.

5 ENDLESS QUESTIONS

It's a known fact that as a child gets older they ask fewer questions and want to contribute less. Year 3s never stop asking questions. Ever. 'Can I sharpen my pencil?' 'What do I do when I get to the end of a page?' 'Can you spell Wednesday?' Again, one simple idea I use is the four Bs: Brain, Buddy, Bits (and Bobs), Boss – I'm last.[1] The children need to go through this list before they talk to me. This took some training and is now getting to the point where I am needed for the little things less. Another idea is to give the children talking/question tokens. Not for every lesson but for when I think they need to go over their thinking and questioning skills.

---

1 For more on 3B4Me (Brain, Book, Buddy, Boss) see: J. Smith, *The Lazy Teacher's Handbook: How Your Students Learn More When You Teach Less* (Carmarthen: Crown House Publishing, 2010), p. 55.

125

6 TA GOLD

This one may be a little out of your control – I have a full-time (almost) teaching assistant who is solid gold. She knows all the children as well as I do and can step up if I'm not there (as the deputy head, I sometimes have to deal with various issues). My teaching assistant works tirelessly at instilling the same rules and ethos as I do and is a great partner to work with. If you have a teaching assistant (part- or full-time) use them well. Ofsted expects it and the children will benefit from them.

> If a Year 3 asks to go to the toilet, let them.

7 TOILETS (PART 2)

One of the endless questions (see tip number 5) I receive is about the toilets. It is frustrating when a child comes to ask me about the toilet if I'm working closely with a group. My class now know they can take themselves to the toilet if there is a spare toilet peg (clothes peg with 'toilet' written on it). This took training and needs constant reminders about expectations and when is *not* an appropriate time to just take themselves off without permission.

8 STORIES

I love reading stories to my class and feel that this is something that gets squeezed out of our timetables. My class love listening to me read and it is something that has a real impact.

They enjoy the voices I use, the over-acting I throw in and the interaction with them. This helps their speaking and listening and, more importantly, their love of reading.

9 CUDDLES

OK, I know this is frowned on; in fact, it's not allowed. I'm 6 foot 5 inches and 16 stone so, compared to my Year 3s, I am, quite literally, a giant. However, getting down to their level and putting an arm around them when they're sad or comforting them when they're hurt is very important. I would want my children's teacher to offer comfort and support to them when they need it.

10 CHECKING: SAYING AND DOING

Just because a Year 3 *says* they've packed that all-important letter in their bag, it doesn't mean they actually have. When they *say* they've checked their tray/locker for their reading diary and can't find it, it doesn't mean they've actually checked. You can have as many systems in place as you like, but sometimes nothing will beat the teacher physically checking. Just do it. From chatting to secondary colleagues, I know this happens with teenagers too!

CHALLENGE

SHAUN ALLISON @SHAUN_ALLISON

1. Have high expectations of all students and expect them all to succeed. Students will always live up to our expectations of them.

2. Have single, challenging learning goals for each lesson – avoid all, most, some objectives as this lowers expectations.

3. Find the 'bright spots', examples of excellent work, during every lesson. Share and discuss with the class what makes it excellent. Stress that this is the standard that students should be aspiring to achieve ... and exceed.

4. Immerse students in excellence from the moment they walk into your room. Display examples of exceptional work all around your classrooms ... and school.

5. Do not accept substandard work. Get students to redraft until they reach the expected standard. Then discuss how they can make it even better!

6. Use peer critique and feedback to encourage students to improve their work and go 'beyond their best'. Watch 'The Story of Austin's Butterfly': http://www.youtube.com/watch?v=hqh1MRWZjms/.

7. Never use the phrase, 'Just do your best', and ban the phrase, 'I'm finished', from your classroom. If students use the phrase, 'I can't do this', follow it up with, 'yet!'

8. Scan the room for students who are stuck – and allow them to stay stuck for a while to build up resilience. Then intervene with questions to get them unstuck and challenge them further.

9. Always include a challenge task that can be accessed by all students at any time during the lesson – one to really stretch and extend their thinking.

10. Plan challenging questions to use throughout the lesson that will stretch and develop deep thinking, but also be responsive and ask questions to develop their thinking, based on their responses.

127

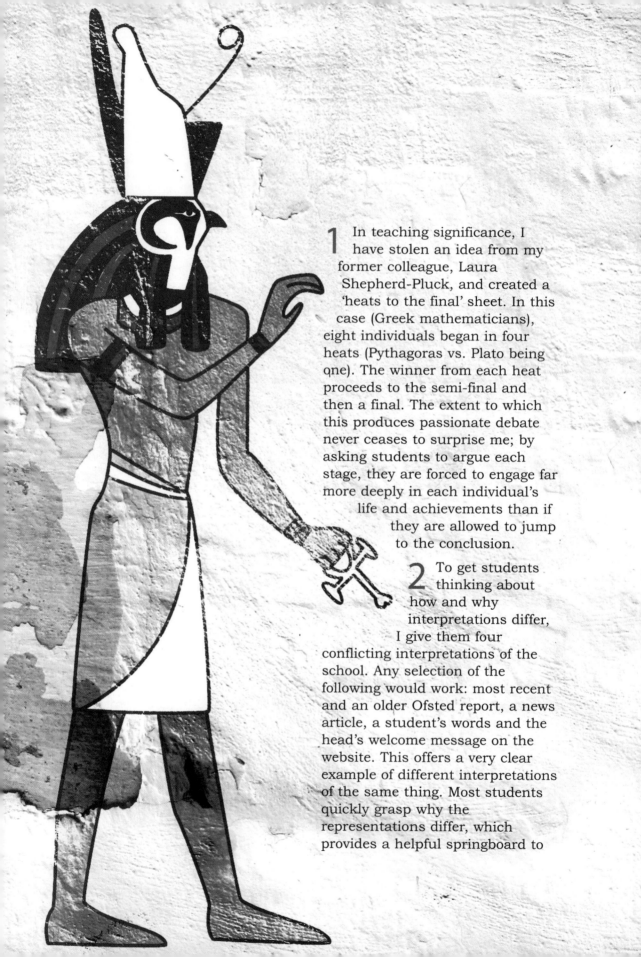

1 In teaching significance, I have stolen an idea from my former colleague, Laura Shepherd-Pluck, and created a 'heats to the final' sheet. In this case (Greek mathematicians), eight individuals began in four heats (Pythagoras vs. Plato being one). The winner from each heat proceeds to the semi-final and then a final. The extent to which this produces passionate debate never ceases to surprise me; by asking students to argue each stage, they are forced to engage far more deeply in each individual's life and achievements than if they are allowed to jump to the conclusion.

2 To get students thinking about how and why interpretations differ, I give them four conflicting interpretations of the school. Any selection of the following would work: most recent and an older Ofsted report, a news article, a student's words and the head's welcome message on the website. This offers a very clear example of different interpretations of the same thing. Most students quickly grasp why the representations differ, which provides a helpful springboard to

HISTORY

HARRY FLETCHER-WOOD @HFLETCHERWOOD

examining other contrasting interpretations. (I know these aren't strictly interpretations, but they provide a good example of the concepts at issue.)

3 I try to make sure students see the relevance of what they're studying; partly to encourage their interest and partly so they value the study of history. A short discussion of how a unit or lesson sheds light on current events or analogous modern problems can be a helpful way to achieve this.

4 I've been thinking more about how I ensure students actually retain what they've learned. Recently, I've been asking students to make their own mnemonics to help commit topics to memory. It seems to work. One which has stuck in my head is 'Naughty Monkeys Are Raiding My Room: I'm Terrified' to remember the order of past societies: Neolithic, Mesopotamian, Ancient Greek, Roman, Middle Ages, Renaissance, Industrial Revolution, Twentieth Century.

5 I use hinge questions to check how much students have understood during the lesson, rather than waiting to discover

they've missed a key point when I'm marking. By giving them a carefully crafted multiple-choice question during the lesson, and getting all the students' answers immediately, I can correct their misconceptions as soon as possible.

6 One of my favourite hooks for a lesson is showing four pictures and asking which is the odd one out. For example, you could use: Kapp, Hitler, Stresemann and Hindenburg. Once you go beyond the superficial (e.g. who has a moustache), students can begin to use their knowledge in creative ways: who died in office? Who never became chancellor? Who fought in the First World War? And so on.

7 I've been experimenting with using 'pre-flight checklists' to help students fix minor errors themselves and better understand what is expected in written work. The students initially peer assess each other's work using the criteria I give them, then use this peer assessment to make amendments to their work. Through the act of peer assessment they identify problems for their peers and gain a clearer idea of what good work should look like for themselves. I need to improve my checklist further, but it seems to help.

8 This year I've taught three units which support what colleagues in other departments

are teaching. I covered the First World War while students read Michael Morpurgo's *Private Peaceful*, slavery and emancipation during their study of Mildred D. Taylor's *Roll of Thunder, Hear My Cry* and the history of maths while they learned about ... the history of maths. From the isolated perspective of my history curriculum this made little sense, but the students benefited hugely, better recognising how subjects can link and showing a deeper understanding of the book, topic and period than would otherwise have been possible. If you don't want to do a whole unit, just a single lesson could have a powerful effect.

9 I recently renewed my lapsed subscription to *Teaching History*. Re-engaging with academic and well-thought-through arguments has helped me to think more deeply about what I'm doing and what good history teaching looks like.

10 This is less of a history-specific tip, but it's an important one nonetheless: start a blog! I've found this to be a huge boost to my teaching, helping me to reflect far more deeply about what I'm doing and how it could be improved. I also feel there are too few blogs by history teachers out there. Perhaps this year could be your year to blog?

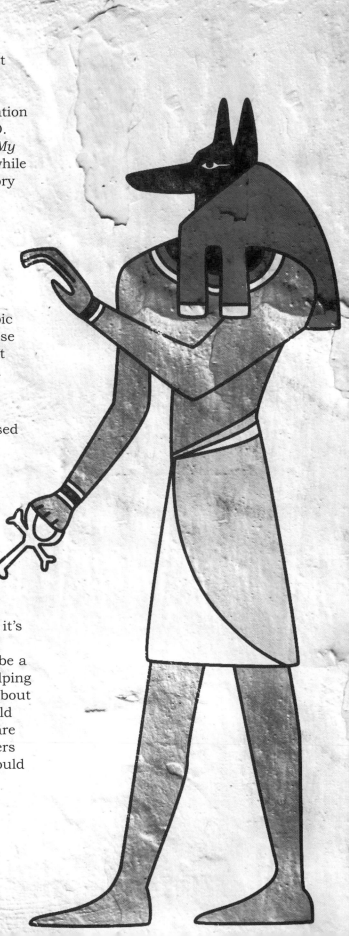

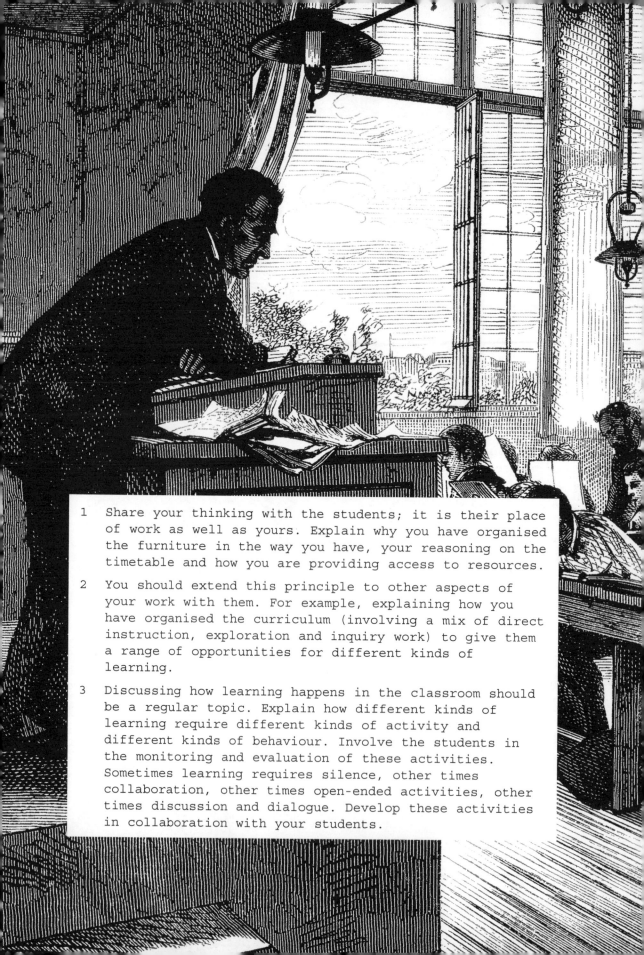

1   Share your thinking with the students; it is their place
    of work as well as yours. Explain why you have organised
    the furniture in the way you have, your reasoning on the
    timetable and how you are providing access to resources.

2   You should extend this principle to other aspects of
    your work with them. For example, explaining how you
    have organised the curriculum (involving a mix of direct
    instruction, exploration and inquiry work) to give them
    a range of opportunities for different kinds of
    learning.

3   Discussing how learning happens in the classroom should
    be a regular topic. Explain how different kinds of
    learning require different kinds of activity and
    different kinds of behaviour. Involve the students in
    the monitoring and evaluation of these activities.
    Sometimes learning requires silence, other times
    collaboration, other times open-ended activities, other
    times discussion and dialogue. Develop these activities
    in collaboration with your students.

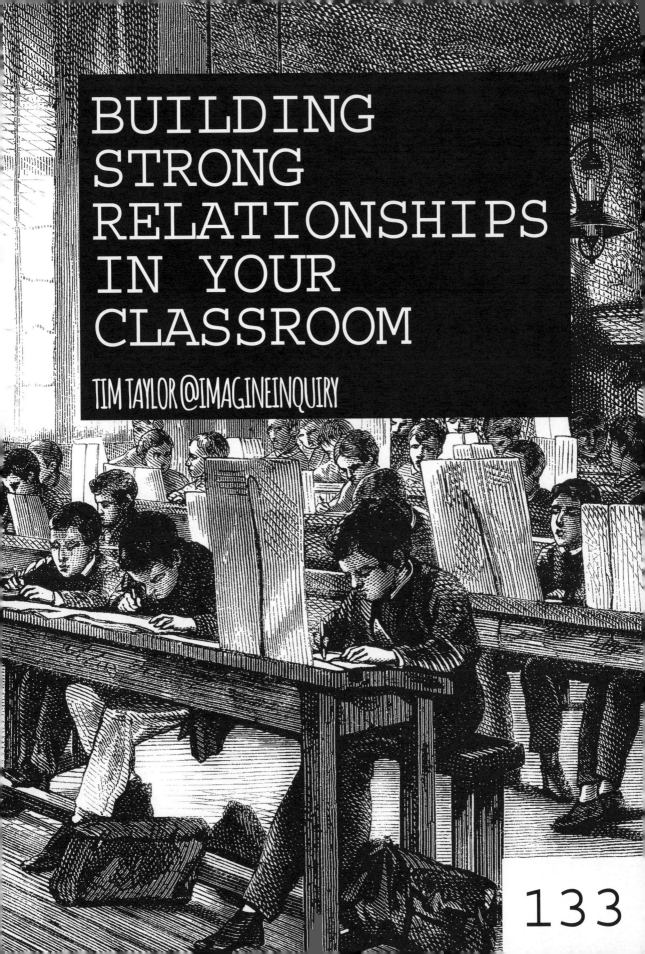

BUILDING STRONG RELATIONSHIPS IN YOUR CLASSROOM

TIM TAYLOR @IMAGINEINQUIRY

133

Discuss new and better ways of doing things, including your own practice. It is called 'practice' for a reason.

4   Talk to your students about the purpose of the curriculum. Why it is organised in the way it is and how you plan to use it to develop their learning. Develop a dialogue in the classroom involving regular student and teacher assessment of how their learning is developing and whether your planning needs to be tweaked and adapted in response.

5   Involve the students in your thinking and evaluation so they can see how learning involves planning, assessment and adaptation.

6   Be honest about your mistakes and discuss with the students how 'mis'-takes are an important part of learning and not something to avoid or hide from.

7   Developing a community of those who try and fail, and then try again, is your main goal: you need to model this. Celebrate your successes together and face up to your mistakes together. Discuss new and better ways of doing things, including your own practice. It is called 'practice' for a reason.

8   The curriculum should consist of two elements:

    i. The prescribed mandatory elements as designated by the national curriculum, the school curriculum and the exam curriculum.

    ii. The emergent non-mandatory elements that are developed and explored by the classroom community as their work develops.

9   Keep in mind these two elements and look for a balance. The students need to understand that the prescribed curriculum is compulsory and non-negotiable (your professional responsibility to teach and their responsibility to learn), but look for opportunities to explore subjects beyond these mandatory elements. Grasp subjects that emerge from your work with them, from the students' own interests, knowledge and passions, and try to weave these into your class curriculum.

10 Although the students are not your friends (and should not be), enjoy your time with them and make learning interesting and fun, but don't lose focus on the purpose. Lesson time is valuable: it is not to be frittered away on nonsense and frivolity. Nevertheless, those who enjoy learning learn better. Strive to engage and excite, to involve and include, to create and transcend. It won't happen every time, but it will never happen at all if you don't try.

MATHS

IESHA SMALL @IESHASMALL

> … don't dumb down. We wouldn't expect a design technology teacher to call a screwdriver 'that pointy thing'

1 HOOK INTO THEIR CURIOSITY

A great first lesson of the year/term for any age group is to ask students to name a mathematical fact or topic that they would like to find out about by the end of the year/term. These can be put in students' books or on a class 'question wall' and ticked off as different areas of the syllabus are covered. They can also be set for homework and develop into an ethos of students building on each other's knowledge

2 BUILD CONFIDENCE

Maths has a reputation for being hard – many people feel that they can't do it and so they give up. As a result they don't practise and a self-perpetuating cycle is created. Establish a safe atmosphere in your classroom, one where it's OK to make mistakes and all mathematical responses (written and spoken) are valued. This will slowly build confidence in even the least sure mathematician and give them the space they need to experiment and make the mistakes that will enable them to improve.

3 USE EVERY OPPORTUNITY TO PRACTISE THE BASICS

It can be tempting to rush through the syllabus but maths is sequential. Make links across areas and don't miss opportunities to reinforce or practise topics that you know your classes struggle with – for example, working with areas is a perfect time to practise multiplication. This can be amended to suit the students: double digits, decimals, mixed units or even algebra (to link to quadratics).

4 USE CORRECT MATHEMATICAL VOCABULARY – DON'T DUMB DOWN

We wouldn't expect a design technology teacher to call a screwdriver 'that pointy thing', but I've seen so many lessons where mathematical terms were dumbed down because teachers felt that the language was too hard for the students. It isn't. They are just words and they represent certain things. Students in the bottom set deserve to know what a coefficient is just as much as those in the top set. Language is powerful: in maths it is very precise, and knowing fancy-sounding terms gives kids confidence (see tip number 2).

5 TAKE A BREAK FROM THE SYLLABUS NOW AND AGAIN

Yes, I said it. The maths syllabus at Key Stages 3 and 4 can be repetitive. Every now and again, find a way to compress the boring bits (e.g. subsume some of the number stuff into a different topic) to do something that excites you for a lesson or two. Yes, I said excites *you*! If it excites you, that passion will translate and your students will feel it and they will be enthused too. Examples? Well, I've spent a lesson with a Year 9 mixed-ability class exploring the world of imaginary numbers and had a Year 11 class debate whether it was fair that Newton got the credit over Leibniz for the differential calculus because of his celebrity at the time.

6 MAKE IT PERSONAL FOR DATA HANDLING/STATISTICS

Like everybody else, students are interested in themselves. Use real data about them to teach statistical topics. Heights and hand spans are favourites. Others can be linked to school foci like attendance data. Don't just stick to your class – compare to others in their year and so on. School censuses are a good resource if you want to use student data and compare to students around the world (see www.censusatschool.org.uk). The Office for National Statistics is also wonderful for raw data. It's possible to search by a local area for data on a range of topics, including social deprivation and crime, and students find this fascinating: http://www.neighbourhood.statistics.gov.uk/dissemination/LeadHome.do?m=0&s=1388685105383&enc=1&ns-js=true&nsck=false&nssvg=false&nswid=1280/.

7   FORGET THE ANSWERS

This seems like an odd thing to say, but in maths students only seem to care about the answer. Teachers moan about this but it is mostly our fault. It is what we condition them to do from very early in their mathematical education. The thought process and working is just as important and, actually, essential when maths is used in context – for example, in the real world in science or engineering. Naturally, on a daily basis, we can insist on showing working out, but to really hammer the point home, every now and again provide the answers and instead turn the task into 'prove this answer is correct'. It's actually standard in the majority of my lessons for me to provide the answers at the start, thereby forcing students to show me their working.

8   TALK TO EVERY SINGLE STUDENT IN EVERY SINGLE LESSON

I teach one-hour lessons with up to 30 in a class. This aids tip number 2 and ensures that nobody becomes invisible. It helps to make sure that you know your students and understand what each and every one can do in each and every lesson. Occasionally it isn't possible, but don't let two lessons go by without having spoken to everybody or asked them a mathematical question. If you need help with allocating your questions, then work your way down or up the register alphabetically or ask students to remind you.

9   WHAT COULD I CHANGE TO MAKE THIS HARDER?

This is a great question for almost any topic and will ensure that you are always challenging your students. Students will come up with all sorts of suggestions: make it negative, add more digits, take a bracket away, change that to a letter and so on. It's non-threatening as you are only asking them to change something, but it can lead to genuinely tough questions that you can then use as extensions or for homework. It's related to the classic 'What if … ?', with the added bonus of the students creating the 'what if' themselves.

10   THROW IN ALGEBRA WHEREVER YOU CAN

This is related to tip number 3. Algebra is pretty much the basis of any higher order mathematics. Students are scared of it, but it can just be considered as taking a specific case and generalising it. Take the fear away from algebra by adding it into other topics on a regular basis. There are many examples of this but Professor John Mason is excellent: http://mcs.open.ac.uk/jhm3/.

> Use every opportunity to practise the basics

DRAMA

HYWEL ROBERTS @HYWEL_ROBERTS

1. There is more to drama than *Glee Club* and making up plays. It's a window on the world; a vehicle of clarity and understanding; a place that trains people in human communication which reinforces tolerance, compromise and empathy, while requiring discipline and self-control. If nothing else, ensure you are teaching these things.

2. Make drama academically *visible* in the profile of your school. Drama is always used in this way (school productions and the like), but what about a Year 8 work in progress evening? Get the parents to value drama as an academic subject. Even if you get just ten parents turning up, it's a start. Give them a brew and show them what you do. Start

intimate and humble, and build from there if you need to.

3. Have learning conversations with other teachers from other subject areas. For example, help each other find the mathematics in drama or the drama in science. See the potential for a blended curriculum using drama as a vehicle for learning and understanding. Make sure you are not the one being precious – see the geography, the physics, the music, the technology in the work you are doing.

> Keep your 'luvvie' in check.

4. Make sure that whatever space you teach in – corridor, canteen, hall, studio – your expectations are clear. Some children find drama challenging and need protecting into it. If the kids are running riot, get them back to basics with clear drama rules and values. Get them hooked in with a prop, an image, a letter, an email, a tattered dress on a hanger.

5. Be an inspiration-seeker. Use your colleagues, Twitter, regional and national drama organisations (e.g. @nateachingdrama and @National_Drama) to build an identity for you and your subject beyond your school. Keep an eye on TeachMeets in your area and get yourself signed up to

contribute. You're a drama teacher! Don't go telling me you can't! Go international and create a blog. Why not? Go to www.wordpress.com and have a play. Show off and share. And read, read, read about the world of education.

6. Keep your 'luvvie' in check. It's endearing for a while, but people might not take you and your subject seriously. Your credibility and that of the subject is important. Challenge the stereotypical image of the drama teacher in the same way many PE teachers have successfully challenged their shell-suited, kid-cropping stereotypes.

7. Make sure the work resonates: if the scheme of work appears childish and isn't resonating with the class you're delivering to, bin it. Create something for the children you have in your school. A mistake some teachers make is to download schemes or projects from the internet that have been written for kids in a private school near Kent, but turn out to be totally hopeless for kids in Barnsley town centre. Ask yourself what the children in your school need to learn and how drama can support this.

8. Build fantastic contexts for your children to learn within. This works in any setting.

Transform the space using imagination – make this the norm. Label the space with sticky notes. Map it out on a big sheet of paper with fat pens. And for those kids who struggle, give them a responsible role. Recently, the basecamp in the forest needed guards on watch. Four boys were excellent when given the role. They needed job descriptions, of course, as well as kitbags ...

9. Make sure you make your lessons BRAVE:

- ■ Buzzing (Did *you* enjoy it? Did they?)

- ■ Relevant (the work and its place in the world)

- ■ Academic (the coverage)

- ■ Vocational (the skills being learned)

- ■ Evaluatory (Have they reviewed their learning?)

> In drama, children can be our best teachers.

This is my checklist which you're very welcome to use. But what about creating your own for you and your team?

10. Drama is one of those subjects that many don't understand, value or see as having rigour. Challenge these assumptions by following tip number 5. If drama becomes one of the key cultural elements in your school, you've done it. Pat yourself on the back and give yourself a round of applause. Then crack on. Be consistent in your expectations. Don't fall into the trap of favouring the kids who *can* do it; challenge those who are intimidated by drama and help them using authentic care and botheredness. Never wing it. And keep learning. In drama, children can be our best teachers.

1 Choose the vehicle for your school blogs carefully and ensure all staff and children understand the 'rules' and 'behaviours' expected when blogging. Devise and agree how this will work in school and when accessing blogs away from school.

RACHEL ORR @RACHELORR

2   Teachers can start simply
    by sharing current and
    future learning with the
    children. For example,
    'Here's what we're going
    to be learning next week',
    can open up the floodgates
    to children undertaking
    some flipped learning
    prior to that week.

3   Engaging children and
    their parents. Something
    as simple as sharing the
    homework, class newsletter
    and so on can draw parents
    in, especially if it's
    difficult to get them
    involved with school life.

FOR TEACHERS
AND STUDENTS

4 Getting started. Begin with something shared that children can contribute to and comment on – for example, a shared story or inviting children to give reasons, suggestions and ideas about something. The possibilities are endless. A picture stimulus can be very open-ended: write a description, what happens next, what happened beforehand. Once you've started you'll find the children can't stop. Projects evolve and reading other blogs will spark off new topics to share and discuss.

5 Ensure teachers always moderate posts and comments before allowing them to go live. Expect the best from children and not just the first words chosen. Let them know when something isn't good enough to be read worldwide.

6 Blogging gets children collaborating, networking and sharing ideas. Develop partner networks for blogging using great projects such as the 100 Word Challenge with @TheHeadsOffice or QuadBlogging with @DeputyMitchell. Share good examples of class blogs from all over the world.

Make your own mark, develop your own style - own it.

7   Encourage the children to comment on each other's work both within class blogs, blogs across the school and those in schools all over the world. There is nothing so powerful as getting feedback from another blogger across the seas. It's a real motivator to get the children writing.

8   Set up a whole-school project moving from class blog to class blog - for example, each class contributing to a school piece of shared writing. One class begins it and hands it on to the next class, which has to read what has been written before continuing. By the end of the project, every class is checking how the writing has developed and is commenting along the way.

9   Open up your audience. Use tags in your blogs and encourage children to tag their blog posts to ensure it reaches the widest audience. As a teacher you suddenly become a teacher of a much larger classroom when sharing blog posts worldwide. Blogs not only offer you the opportunity to share your ideas but also to collect ideas, suggestions or answers to questions.

10 Be creative in your blog - use images, links, audio, video clips. Make your own mark, develop your own style - own it.

COMPUTING FOR PRIMARY

MARTIN BURRETT @ICTMAGIC

In the primary school, where tech support is often fleeting or missing altogether, the rules for ICT are very different. Teachers are often on their own, pitting their wits against a moody school network, and a war mentality is often the result. But it doesn't have to be this way. These top ten tips will help you avoid problems and cope with them should they occur.

1 BE PREPARED

It may sound obvious, but it is important to try out whatever it is you are planning to do in class before you present it to the children. I liken this to playing music. Most teachers would look over the music briefly before playing in front of an audience. To further the analogy, beginners to computing are similar to new musicians in that they will be able to pick up their instrument and struggle through a slow rendition of 'Frère Jacques', but there will be plenty of squeaks and wincing along the way. Using technology well is a skill and one that requires time to learn.

Test things out that you haven't used before. That wonderful website you found at home may be brilliant but it may not work at school, so forward planning is essential. If your school's network security settings are different for teachers and students, it is also a good idea to check any website on a pupil's account if you plan to ask the children to use it.

Never work without a safety net. Even the most prepared teacher can still be left with a crashed network or a power cut, so you should try to plan an alternative activity for when the technology lets you down. If possible, try to make this task something the children can do independently so you can try to fix the problem. I distain 'filler work', so make sure the task is useful and

> Never work without a safety net … you should try to plan an alternative activity for when the technology lets you down.

fun. The kids are missing out on fun time on the computers, after all!

2 BE INDEPENDENT

A computer network has the power to stop your class getting online, but the same should not be true of you. All teachers should have a means of accessing the web independently which bypasses the school network. You should be able to use your mobile phone to tether a computer and use it like a portable modem via a USB cable. Most modern smartphones allow you to create a wireless hotspot which can provide web access to three or four computers at a reasonable speed. However, this will use up your data allowance so you will need to be careful that you do not incur charges.

You can buy devices that are designed specifically for this purpose. You may wish to purchase an internet dongle (yes, that is a thing!) which goes into your computer's USB slot and then uses the mobile phone network to provide web access. You can also buy a portable wireless hub or 'Mi-Fi', which again will give you good internet speeds for around three or four computers. I strongly recommend that every school buys a few portable wireless hubs as they are superb for field trips and outside learning.

Finally, you may be lucky enough to have residential areas or businesses close by your classroom. You may be able to access BT's open network (other telecom companies are available). This is free to access for BT broadband users and fairly priced for everyone else. Look for BT Wi-Fi in your choice of networks.

3   FREE ADVICE

Money can be hard to come by in education. But luckily the web is awash with a myriad of free tools to improve the teaching and learning in your school, so you can save your funds for other things.

A large yearly expense for many schools is maintaining a learning platform, but there are a growing number of free platforms where you can set up a functional online environment for both teachers and pupils to use. Google Apps for Education is one of the most popular of these platforms, which draws on tools like Gmail, Google sites, Drive and many more to make a superb collaborative suite of tools. http://edmodo.com provides some of the same functions in a simpler way.

Software can also be costly for schools. A little research can save you a fortune by providing you with free alternatives to expensive educational tools. When looking for free sites and tools to use in your class, a good start is to ask the educational community on Twitter if they know of websites which can cater for your needs. It never ceases to amaze me how resourceful and helpful these educators can be.

> … the web is awash with a myriad of free tools to improve the teaching and learning in your school

Check out the #UKEdChat hashtag to find these amazing educators.

Two other places I find invaluable for discovering useful resources are www.scoop.it and www.pinterest.com, where users share eclectic items of interest. Just enter the search term or follow interesting educators to find great resources for your class.

There are many educators who have made it their mission to collect and share wonderful resources on their websites. There are far too many sites to mention, but three of my current favourites are www.makeuseof.com, www.freetech4teachers.com and http://kbkonnected.tumblr.com. The collaborative power of the crowd is immense. Make sure your class benefits from it.

4   BEFRIEND YOUR INTERNET SECURITY MANAGER

Most school web security settings are more sensitive than a child who forgot it was a non-uniform day. They block everything with an impenetrable stubbornness, yet many of these sites would provide wonderful learning opportunities. Most security providers allow you to unblock sites when you request them to do so, so make sure you find the right person to contact. This is often written on the block screen. Plan ahead, as it can take a while for your request to be acted on.

5   WINDOW TO THE WORLD

Your school website is a wonderful way to communicate with the school community. It provides an easy way for parents to find information and show off the amazing things that your children do in class. But they should be adaptive and updated constantly to really add something useful to the life of the school. There are various ways to make your website more responsive. Many schools use a blog to post updates to their websites in seconds, with an increasing number of schools turning responsibility to maintain this over to the pupils. If you have the skills in your school community, it is even better to bring the website 'in house'.

> Most school web security settings are more sensitive than a child who forgot it was a non-uniform day.

6   STORAGE

First they were huge, then they were floppy, next came the sticks, but all storage devices have similar problems. They are easy to lose and they do not fare well after a spin cycle. But more and more teachers are leaving physical storage devices behind and storing all their files online in 'the cloud'. Free services like www.dropbox.com and www.copy.com have made saving items to the web as easy as saving into a folder. Once your files are there you can access them via any web-enabled device. If you regularly lose files to digital gremlins, you have the peace of mind that versions of your files are stored and can be restored easily.

7   GET OUTSIDE

Tech looks lovely when it is lined up in rows in a computer suite or on a trolley, but ultimately it is a tool with which to create and explore. While much of this can be done within the classroom, it is amazing to see how your pupils will use tech outside. The 'adventure' may be a small trip into the school library to research some aspect of the books or taking recording equipment into the school kitchens to interrogate the staff about the true contents of their shepherd's pie, but taking your learning out of the artificial environment of the classroom can have great rewards. Naturally, I am not suggesting that you take your aging desktops for a lap of the park, but mobile tech is everywhere and not always expensive. Audio recorders are inexpensive these days and basic cameras that can shoot photos and reasonable video can be bought and replaced for around £20 when little Jonny tests their water-resistant capabilities.

8   SET UP AND STEP BACK

As educators we often find it difficult to step back and allow our children to struggle a little – it is our instinct to help. But if you can set up a suitably levelled goal, the children can use their ingenuity and previously acquired skills to work things out to achieve it. We need to let go of the idea that there is a particular way to create something or solve a problem and let the children figure it out for themselves. There will be times when you will need to show the children how to do something and you should try to spot these potential hurdles ahead of time so you are prepared, but use your 'little technicians' to help other children wherever possible rather than you doing it for them.

9   LEADING THE WAY

There are those children who seem to speak binary and have silicon embedded in their fingertips. These are the children who relish technology and can achieve unbelievable things for their age. Utilise their knowledge, skill and passion as digital leaders. Digital leaders are a group of skilled and interested pupils who help with technology across the school. Their roles vary from school to school, but their main job is to support teachers and their peers when necessary. The digital leaders usually receive extra technological tutorage during lunchtimes or breaktimes, and they are encouraged to explore the digital world during their own time and

> Digital leaders are a group of skilled and interested pupils who help with technology across the school.

report back and teach other digital leaders about what they have discovered. They will be a wonderful asset to your school.

10   BE BOLD

Technology will frustrate you. It will ruin lessons and make you use language that even a spell-checker can't clean up. But the opportunities and possible discoveries that technology affords us as educators and learners make the teething troubles (just about) bearable. Technology allows us to surround our children with insights that would have been impossible just a generation ago. So be bold, move away from the idea that technology in the classroom is novel, aim high and embed technology into your teaching. Try new things, fail occasionally, but grow in your knowledge and experience along the way. Both you and your class will be thankful if you do.

As I see it, a bottom-up approach is not a do-what-you-like free-for-all. It is never a case of anything goes. It relies on clear and distinct structures, including line management, professional development policies and classroom expectations.

BOTTOM-UP LEADERSHIP

KEV BARTLE @KEVBARTLE

1 FOCUS ON YOUR SURPLUSES, NOT YOUR DEFICITS

A bottom-up approach to school leadership needs to be built on what each person in the organisation can do well. The days of the negatively focused 'deficit audit' need to be consigned to the dustbin of history. And guess what? If you ask people to start with what they do well, they are much more likely to feel confident in drawing from the surpluses of others in addressing their own deficits.

2 PLACE COMPLETE TRUST IN YOUR COLLEAGUES

Remember that the vast majority of people who enter the world of education are in it because of a sense of moral purpose, not in order to achieve power, make themselves rich or travel the world. Hold that thought close as you hand over decision-making powers to them. Have belief in their capacity to do things just as well as a member of the SLT, and show them that you have faith by leaving them to it and supporting or challenging them from a distance.

3 SEE BEYOND YOUR ASPIRATIONAL MIDDLE LEADERS

Some so-called bottom-up approaches are actually little more than middle-down, with the distribution/delegation of responsibility to trusted middle leaders. If you want a genuine bottom-up approach, you need to reach out to the classroom practitioners from among your staff, not just the next generation of SLT, although this could cause friction with middle leaders. If you don't do this, then you will be seen as simply passing the buck of responsibility, not empowering others.

4 EMBRACE THE DISEQUILIBRIUM THAT ENSUES

A bottom-up approach involves widening the spectrum of participation and so it is inevitable that, given real responsibility, the Trojan mouse among your staff will do things that turn what you have always thought about school leadership on its head. It will feel distinctly uncomfortable not doing it all yourself (as SLT like to do), but you have to go with the flow and enjoy the giddiness of the ride. Plant a smile on your face and wait until you realise that you're not forcing it any more.

5 BE AGILE AND DON'T WORRY TOO MUCH ABOUT PLANS

The top-down approach favoured by schools leads to hugely bureaucratic improvement planning structures (for schools, teams and individuals) in which each action is carefully planned and sequenced. A bottom-up approach is much more responsive. It still needs a sense of vision and some end goals, but the planned pathway splits and twists and gets blocked on frequent occasions. When it does, change the plan and don't lose sleep over the one you have just abandoned.

6   BECOME A SERENDIPITY SPOTTER

Following on from the previous point, sometimes a committedly bottom-up leader needs to not wait for the path to split, twist or get blocked. Sometimes you need to split, twist or block it deliberately yourself because you (or one of the Trojan mice at your school) have stumbled across something that just screams to be included in your work. Don't fight this feeling. Learn to look out of the corner of your leadership eye for those opportunities that simply don't come at you head-on.

7   CREATE THE CONDITIONS FOR CONNECTIONS

Leadership of teaching and learning by classroom practitioners requires that they have the opportunities to connect with one another and with others in the field of education. Do everything you can to give teachers time together on INSET days, develop a school blogsite, encourage the use of Twitter and create a spirit of ongoing dialogue. But don't expect every conversation to be obviously 'productive'. Phatic communication , strengthens the bonds that, in turn, bring about 'productivity', and this can never be forced into being.

8   KEEP THE RULES SIMPLE

As I see it, a bottom-up approach is not a do-what-you-like free-for-all. It is never a case of anything goes. It relies on clear and distinct structures, including line management, professional development policies and classroom expectations. But, in the same way as the safety net in a circus allows trapeze artists to do amazing things, so a clear set of simple but emphatic policies and procedures allows staff at your school to lead teaching and learning in a coherent and focused manner.

9   DON'T PANIC WHEN THINGS GO WRONG

If you want your school's approach to teaching and learning to be clinically efficient, then a bottom-up approach just isn't for you. A genuinely distributed pedagogy will be messy and will fail almost as often as it succeeds, but it will also learn from its mistakes, and so will those who lead it. Too many of us on SLTs suffer from a 'hero complex' and will jump in to save the day at the first sign of trouble. Pack away your external underpants, Superman, and let the damsels save themselves.

10   NEVER TRY TO ROLL THINGS OUT EN MASSE

Perhaps the most important piece of advice has been left until the very end. If you have followed all of the above guidance and discovered that a genuinely brilliant thing has happened in one of your classrooms as a result, avoid thinking that this can simply be 'scaled up' to all classrooms. Instead, nudge others to look, listen, learn and perhaps even have a try of it, but don't take it along to the hall for your next INSET day. That kind of behaviour is just not bottom-up, my friend.

1   Students aren't puppets and will behave in ways you will
    not have planned for or predicted. Sometimes this can be
    absolutely joyous and sometimes it can be absolutely
    horrible. Be brave enough to see where it takes you when
    it's joyous. Be brave enough to forgive yourself when
    it's not.

2   Good relationships are key with both students and staff.
    Try to do your utmost to maintain them. Having said
    that, don't be anyone's doormat.

3   Carry many, many pens. Pound shops are your friend.

4   A large amount of paperwork is a feature of the job.
    Learn to accept this. Work hard on efficient marking and
    admin routines even if it means staying on for a bit.
    Your home should be a refuge from, not an extension of,
    your working life. This is easier to write about than
    do. Believe me, I know.

5   I don't care how old they are, behaviour management
    must be a priority. Accept nothing but the highest of
    standards. This does not mean you have to be a
    prison warden.

6   Trust in the classroom is extremely important and it
    works both ways. If you say you are going to do
    something, do it. If not, don't expect them to.

7   Technology in education should be there to help you and
    your students. If it doesn't, there is absolutely no
    point in its inclusion. Also, if your classrooms have
    ceiling-mounted projectors, buy a universal remote
    for them. It will save you a lot of searching in the
    long run.

8   Use humour when you can. If you make them laugh they'll
    be more inclined to listen to what you say. Fear can
    also be a great motivational tool. Use both at your
    discretion, but do not disregard either.

9   Clean the whiteboard when you finish the lesson. This is
    the smallest courtesy you can pay to someone who may be
    using the room after you and gets right on my last nerve
    when it doesn't happen.

10 There are a multitude of factors that can affect a
    student. Do not assume something they do is directly
    down to something you did.

> Be brave enough to see where it takes you when it's joyous. Be brave enough to forgive yourself when it's not.

POST-COMPULSORY LEARNING

THOMAS STARKEY @TSTARKEY1212

Too often we pitch to the middle,
have an extension for the top and
a scaffold for the bottom.

**What if all your students had the
chance to try to get to the top?**

PEDAGOGY

DEBBIE AND MEL @TEACHERTWEAKS

1 Have the highest expectations of all of your students. They will constantly surprise you in what they can do, as long as they are encouraged to achieve, the task is suitably challenging and there are appropriate resources. Too often we pitch to the middle, have an extension for the top and a scaffold for the bottom. What if all your students had the chance to try to get to the top? Don't be the one to put a ceiling on them. The best differentiation is knowing your students really well, so you know the best ways to support all of them to keep on learning even when it becomes really tough.

2 Providing exemplars for students is so important if they are to know what excellence looks like in your subject. When showing exemplars, give students time to talk through what makes them excellent so everyone has a really clear picture of this before they start on their own work. Once students know what excellence looks like, they will be able to judge with greater accuracy how their work and the work of their peers is shaping up during a series of lessons.

3 Begin your planning by asking yourself what you want them to learn and then how you will judge if they have learned it or not. Plan for learning to take place rather than plan over-elaborate tasks that look good superficially but don't really allow students to think deeply, or find something difficult that will make them feel proud when they grasp something out of their comfort zone.

4 The most powerful tool we have as teachers is our ability to ask the right type of questions. Are you using them well? Questions should be used to check understanding, to clarify new ideas and concepts, to get students to think, to spark off a debate and to help students reflect on what they're learning. Plan in advance the questions you want to ask and have an idea of how you will target particular students who may need more prodding than others. Keep a log of great questions your students ask, share them with other students and jot down when a question you've asked has had a positive response.

5 Often, we forget how difficult students find it to have effective discussion with their peers. Yes, some students may like to talk a lot, but that doesn't mean they have all learned the social rules or have the academic language to hold their own in a discussion. Teach them explicitly how to participate in discussions by modelling the academic language required and provide a range of question stems to help students know how to begin.

6 When planning what to teach, don't forget to plan how and when you will be assessing the students. It's so easy to mismanage this and end up with three marking deadlines in the same week. Aim to mark little and often and give your students adequate time to respond to your feedback. There are many different ways to mark, but decide early on what your way will be and how you will

communicate this to the students. Stick to the same method of marking so students are crystal clear on the feedback you are giving them. The sooner they get used to your way of marking, the sooner they will be able to engage in some sort of dialogue with you.

7 When a student enters your classroom, what kind of environment are they walking into? If you are lucky enough to have your own classroom, make it a space to be proud of – it is an extension of you. What you value should be projected onto your classroom walls. Have an achievement wall, which students are pleased to be on if they've done something to be proud of, have a space for students to write questions about a topic they're studying or where they can leave comments for their peers, and have displays of exemplar work or helpful stimuli for students.

> If you are lucky enough to have your own classroom, make it a space to be proud of – it is an extension of you.

8 Sometimes it's OK to rip up the lesson plan and go off in a different direction. Some of the best lessons we've had were completely unexpected. A student asks a question you weren't expecting and the class become animated and discussion flows. Something

you thought you'd explained well ends up with confused faces 20 minutes later so you take a step back and do some really effective modelling to get the class back on track. An anecdote to help your class understand something new turns into a full-blown story. We could go on and on with our unplanned moments that turned into great learning episodes. The point is: let go of the reins sometimes and see what happens!

9 As we all know, teaching can be the most time-consuming of jobs and the idea of a work–life balance can go out of the window at certain pressure points in the calendar. Teaching can be isolating but don't fall into that trap – get out there and ask colleagues what resources they've used and reciprocate by sharing what you've got. Often we don't share our resources because we talk ourselves into thinking that people have probably got better things than we do, but you never know how useful something might be until you use it. Yes, you will most likely tweak strategies for the students you have sitting in front of you, but it's better than starting from scratch with every class. So, next time you see a wild-eyed colleague staring at a computer screen or manically flicking through a textbook, ask them what they need and see if you can help!

10 Last, but by no means least, join Twitter. This links to tip number 9 about being part of a teaching community where we try to help each other out as much as possible. It's important to have some clear pedagogical beliefs – otherwise you'll end up doing all sorts without really knowing why. However, to become a great teacher, you should look to challenge your beliefs to see if they hold up to serious challenge. If they do, great. If they wobble, then it's time to reflect and think what you can do to become the best teacher you can be. Set aside time during the week to read some of the brilliant blogs out there on Twitter. Subscribe to them and you'll get an email notification, so you'll be sure not to miss anything fabulous!

... next time you see a wild-eyed colleague staring at a computer screen or manically flicking through a textbook, **ask them what they need and see if you can help!**

enthuse the students
- share with them
your passion for the
subject. Fire up their
imaginations.

ENJOY TEACHING ART

JO BAKER @JOBAKER9

1 **ENCOURAGE CONFIDENCE**. Try to instil a sense of confidence in your students. You need to nurture an environment where it is OK for things to go wrong. You must also enthuse the students – share with them your passion for the subject. Fire up their imaginations. Smile – you set the scene inside the class. You are the conductor. Enthuse and celebrate the students' work. Highlight success, no matter how small. It is these tiny things which build confidence, enthusiasm and resilience in your students.

2 **CHANGE YOUR SCHEMES OF WORK REGULARLY**. Take risks, be inspiring and be willing to adapt/alter the schemes at a moment's notice. Ask for students'

opinions – they can help co-design schemes with you. Students will invest far more into a project that they have helped to design. This helps to keep your schemes relevant and current. Encourage students to use the technology they have in their pockets. Continually push yourself out of your comfort zone.

3 **DEMONSTRATIONS**. Invest time in creating quality demonstrations/examples. Set high standards. Inspire the students – show them what they could achieve. You could record some video while you create the examples for students to use as a visual reference for each stage. Model good techniques but realise that your way is not the only way!

163

4   **AN ABSOLUTE MUST: ESTABLISH CLEAR ROUTINES AND EXPECTATIONS**. Tidy-up time can be a real nightmare so you must take time to create clear routines. A few rules set out at the beginning of the year will pay dividends. Be clear, concise and do not accept silliness or sloppy cleaning. Insist on high standards - these will rub off on your students. I always clear away to music - I estimate the pack-up time needed and choose a song accordingly. Students must be finished and sat down by the end of the song. I use a range from *Countdown*'s 30-second theme to the *Mission: Impossible* music (old TV series for shorter, new film version for longer) or Bizet's *Carmen*. All get the students focused on the job at hand.

> A few rules set out at the beginning of the year will pay dividends.

5   **DISPLAY IS VITAL**. Open up your students' work to a wider audience. Set up a department Twitter account and blog to display your students' work. I have been amazed at the difference opening up my students' work to a global audience has had on them. It has encouraged them to take a real pride in their work. Celebrate it with them. Organise exhibitions, display work in your classroom, in the corridors - anywhere you can find to showcase the work. A board set up behind you at parents' evening will create a mini exhibition space, highlighting the wonderful work going on. Search out prime display space within your school, but the ultimate space is the classroom - make it look amazing.

6   **NETWORK**. Be an outward-facing department. Be inspired by others. Share ideas. Network and forge relationships with local galleries, museums, designers and craftspeople. Search out grants and funding, arrange for artists in residence if you can. Ask the local gallery if they have a work loan programme - many will bring work into school for your students to view.

7 CONTINUE TO MAKE YOUR OWN ARTWORK – INSIDE AND OUTSIDE THE CLASSROOM. Put into practice what you preach. Let it inspire students to help them create their own. Let them see the mistakes you make – discuss them. Model the work you are asking them to do. Inspire, encourage – but offer your way as just one option. Take stock, reflect and review regularly – and encourage your students to do the same. Not just in your artwork but throughout your teaching.

> Befriend the support staff. … Treat your cleaner like royalty.

8 BEFRIEND THE SUPPORT STAFF. They will prove invaluable. Treat your cleaner like royalty.

9 ENCOURAGE CREATIVITY. Talk to students about their work, plans and ideas. Understand the motivation behind them. You will be surprised at how much you learn from the students. Do not try to have them all doing exactly what you have done. They are artists when they enter your room – believe in them, and they will believe in themselves.

10 ESTABLISH SKILLS-BASED PROJECTS IN THE EARLY YEARS in order for later project-based learning to be successful and innovative. For students to be confident, creative and daring artists, they need to have a broad skills base. The world is their oyster once they have mastered the basics. This also instils confidence and a wider variety of work at GCSE and A level, where your priority can be developing ideas and creativity rather than just focusing on skills.

ORGANISING AN EDU-EVENT

Keep the focus clear, simple and prominent and the day will be a huge success.

1 Have a clear purpose for the event. What do you hope to achieve? What is the aim? It is important that the event you are organising has a clear focus. It helps to clarify what it is that you are trying to get out of the day. With a focal point in mind, you can then plan as best as possible to ensure

that the focus and ethos is driven throughout and after the event. At #TLT13, for example, the aim was to concentrate on the main areas of classroom practice, such as feedback, planning and questioning, and allow as much discussion as possible on these areas throughout the day. Having such a clear focus

also ensures that the public are well informed about what to expect and it will attract those who are truly interested in attending. Keep the focus clear, simple and prominent and the day will be a huge success.

2 Select a great venue or space that meets the needs of the day. It doesn't need to be big and grand, just make the event run well. You don't need a glamorous setting to have a successful day. Many excellent events are set in unusual spaces. However, it is important that you choose a venue that meets the

needs of your event. Is it easily accessible for delegates? Are there good transport links for those not travelling by car? If it is a big event, are there local hotels and so on that could accommodate those who are staying overnight? Are there enough rooms or spaces for the various presenters or workshops? What is the maximum capacity? Will the venue feel cramped or overcrowded if you get the number of delegates you want? Does the venue have any catering facilities? Does it have IT equipment for presentations? Is there Wi-Fi available for delegates to sign up to? Questions like these should help you to ascertain whether the venue you are choosing is the right place for your day. You may not get it all right at first go, but it's a good place to start!

3 Communication is key. Before, during and after, keep everyone (delegates, speakers, venue) informed. There are so many effective ways to keep communication clear in the modern era. Social media, such as Twitter or Facebook, means that your event can be advertised to as many people as possible. Creating a webpage or WordPress site to direct people to can ensure you keep all the relevant information in the same place. Using a mailing list in the run-up to the event means that you can contact potential delegates easily. The aim is to make sure that everyone who wishes to attend the event is as well informed as possible. A welcoming feel to the day can be a winner and will make your event feel both personal and professional.

> Communication is key. Before, during and after, keep everyone informed.

Don't forget to keep in regular contact with the presenters and the venue. Checking in and seeing what needs or requests they have can ensure any blips are kept to the minimum. Explain logistics in a very structured and methodical way so everyone behind the scenes feels comfortable and stress-free. If possible, visit the venue and explain exactly what you want and pose as many questions as you can. Developing a contact who knows exactly what you want will ensure that the day is trouble-free.

4 Create excitement! We did this through Twitter. We hyped up #TLT13 and the tickets sold out in one week as a result. It sounds silly but creating a buzz about the event beforehand ensures the day catches people's attention. We started a quick yet effective publicity campaign in the run-up to releasing tickets. The numerous 'teaser tweets' and 'something is happening ... Saturday 19 October' messages caught people's attention and got them talking. When we released the sign-up, the response was overwhelming. Get that buzz going!

5 Have systems in place to make life easier! An event is quite a logistical job – there are many tasks and admin duties that need to be tackled. There are various websites, platforms and pieces of software that can decrease your workload. WordPress can sort out a web page. Eventbrite can sort ticket sales and allocation. Google Docs can make session sign-ups stress free. Surf the

internet, investigate what is out there and use whatever will make the organisation as easy as possible.

6 Prepare for the worst (people dropping out, room changes, etc.) and always have back-up plans. Unfortunately things do go wrong. If you have systems in place these problems can be dealt with more easily. For example, what happens if you don't get the numbers attending? What happens if the date has to be moved? What happens if there is a problem at the venue beforehand? What if technology fails on the day? Think about the worst-case scenarios and calmly consider what you could do as an alternative.

7 Get some really great speakers. You can create the biggest buzz in the world but you need to make sure your day has substance. Carefully select some fantastic people to speak. Delegates are there to learn new things or to be challenged. If your presenters can't do that, then it might be worth searching for some replacements.

8 Keep it tight but loose. We had different categories/themes for the workshops but gave leaders the freedom to plan what they wanted. Give your presenters some leeway but have clear guidelines. We had a number of simple expectations (e.g. there must be time in sessions for discussion and collaboration). After this, presenters were allowed the creative freedom to design their workshop however they wished. As a result, we had presenters who felt relaxed and got as much from the day as the delegates did.

> Give your presenters some leeway but have clear guidelines

9 Involve the delegates. We had TeachMeet workshops and a Genius Bar so attendees were involved throughout. We all hate being talked at for hours on end, so think about what you would want from an event like yours. Get the delegates involved as much as possible so they can leave feeling that they have been truly immersed in the ethos of the day. Whatever you do, ensure there is time for discussion and chat. The speakers are the catalysts, but the delegates are the lifeblood of events like this.

10 Make your event's presence felt and your message continue long after the sun has set on the day itself. Depending on your location, the time of year or merely restrictions on size, if you have created an interest in your event there will inevitably be those who cannot attend. Delegates are brilliant at sharing ideas in their schools, through Twitter and blog posts, but it's a good idea to find ways of disseminating the ideas after the event. You may wish to upload videos to YouTube or, as we did, create a document with links and guides to presenters, topics and workshop information. This is rather time consuming but a good way to reflect on your event, to remind yourself of the highs and lows and to share everyone's hard work with as many people as possible. This may also help encourage people to attend a future event should you choose, in a moment of madness, to run another one!

1. When planning lessons ask yourself two questions:
   i. What impact does this activity have on knowledge and understanding?
   ii. How does this activity deepen learning?

   This way you will always plan appropriate learning activities for your pupils which support, stretch and challenge them.

2. Spend some time teaching sound/spelling links and how to apply them. Then give the pupils plenty of practice at the beginning of each lesson to build confidence and encourage independence with pronunciation and listening skills.

3. When tackling more challenging listening tasks, always give pupils the transcripts as this will help them to separate out sound/spelling links and words. If starting on a new topic, use the transcripts to work through vocabulary and grammar structures before tackling the actual listening activities to build confidence, knowledge and understanding.

4. Teach dictionary skills early on so pupils know how to look up vocabulary and use grammar terminology. Teach them the problems with internet translators and train pupils to use sites such as www. wordreference.com instead.

5. When setting homework, give pupils core and independent work which also includes vocabulary manipulation tasks. Aim to give timescales for completion of core tasks and clear rewards for any extra independent work done. Try to build in some project work (using vocabulary) with a choice of presentation forms, alongside the more formal homework tasks, to encourage pupils to spend more time on their MFL work.

6. Help pupils to cut down on their learning by teaching the rules and then any exceptions to them. Get them to master the exceptions so that they learn around a few pieces of

MODERN LANGUAGES

JAN BAKER @JANBAKER97

vocabulary instead of trying to learn all of it.

7. Encourage pupils to listen to target language radio stations when doing other things (e.g. while cleaning their bedroom). This will get them used to the rhythm of the language and listening tasks will sound a lot slower in class which will help their confidence. Let them know that they are not expected to understand everything they are listening to so that they are not too discouraged.

8. Wherever possible give pupils reasons to use the target language. Find pen pals, link with other schools or employ foreign language assistants. In the age of Skype and instant messaging, linking with other language speakers shouldn't be difficult. Use the British Council website as a starting point for finding compatible schools if necessary. Find out if you have local companies who have foreign language speaking skills/native speakers and invite them in to work with pupils.

9. Create a climate in your classroom where pupils are not afraid to try and don't feel foolish if they make mistakes. Explain that mistakes give everyone the opportunity to revisit the learning. If pupils do badly in an assessment, and you want to build their confidence, allow them to re-sit the assessment with the proviso that the minimum expected mark is 50% and watch their confidence grow when they achieve more the second time around.

10. Teach memory and 'how to learn vocabulary' techniques and incorporate these into your teaching from day one. Look at your assessments and plan to introduce GCSE-style assessments at Key Stage 3 so pupils are aware and have had practice completing them before they choose their options. This way they will know what to expect and will have had some success at GCSE-type tasks before they begin the course.

1. You differentiate all the time, so become more aware of all the subconscious strategies you use. Whenever you adapt what you teach or how you teach it for an individual child, that is differentiation.

2. Get into the habit of 'topping' and 'tailing' the activities you use – think of a potential extension and a potential support.

3. You can differentiate the way you talk to your students by saying the same thing in different ways – once in a simple form and again using more complex vocabulary.

4. Adapt the length of time you give for students to do tasks to increase the level of challenge. Experiment with short time limits to create a sense of pace.

5. Think beyond the classroom – give students access to a tricky text to read before a lesson or set a long-term project to enrich and broaden their experiences.

DIFFERENTIATION

SUE COWLEY @SUE_COWLEY

6 To differentiate you have to know your students: view every interaction you have with them as a chance to get to know them better.

7 Use different ways of grouping students to increase differentiation - for instance, grouping by reading age.

8 Find activities that can be accessed at various different levels, ones that naturally lend themselves to differentiation.

9 Sometimes offer a choice of formats in which to complete a task so that the students have a sense of control over their own learning.

10 Use resources in a creative way to appeal to different kinds of learners and to inspire imaginative thinking.

... we often forget that the
reason some teaching methods
have lasted for centuries
is because they work.

TEN THINGS OFSTED WON'T LIKE

ANDREW OLD @OLDANDREWUK

In a teaching world where the latest fashion is aggressively promoted and Ofsted is always condemning teachers for actually teaching their classes, we often forget that the reason some teaching methods have lasted for centuries is because they work. Here are a number of things you should try, just try, to see for yourself whether they work or not, even if you have been told for years that they don't and even if you have mistakenly (and, I assure you, it is mistakenly) assumed that the research shows they don't.

1 SIT STUDENTS IN ROWS

It turns out that if students can see and hear the one person in the room who is an expert in what they are learning, rather than the faces of other children, then they often learn more through paying more attention to what is being taught. It also means that it is obvious if students are holding conversations when they should be listening. They can always turn around for group work, but they will learn more from a good teacher than from their peers, so that should be the default.

2 FLICK AND TICK MARKING

I don't mean literally 'flicking' – do pay attention – but I do mean marking that is done quickly and with little more than ticks, crosses and the occasional 'well done' or 'not enough' when required. I'm not disputing that sophisticated systems of diagnostic marking and target setting are more effective and should be used as well, but flick and tick is often the most efficient use of your time. If you demonstrate to students that you are looking at their books regularly, and that you will notice when they are working well and when

they aren't, then it will impact on their behaviour and effort, and that is time well spent. If a marking policy means that you'll only have time to mark every four months, ignore it and get ticking.

3 TEACH FACTS

Few things are more derided in education than the teaching of facts. Often the word 'facts' is used as a derogatory term for the teaching of knowledge. We now know that knowledge is a key part of virtually all thinking and, to that extent, knowledge has been rehabilitated. But, partly, we tend to marginalise facts in order to emphasise that knowledge is more than facts, and that it includes ideas, understanding and whole systems of thought. So, why I am defending facts? Well, a fact is usually knowledge reduced to a single statement, and single statements are often easier to absorb and understand than complex ideas. A good first step (and this is only the first step) in teaching knowledge (and therefore thinking) is to see if you can reduce that knowledge to key statements to be remembered, i.e. facts. As long as the introduction of facts is seen as the first step to knowledge, and recall of facts is not seen as the ultimate end of education, then we should be unashamed to teach facts.

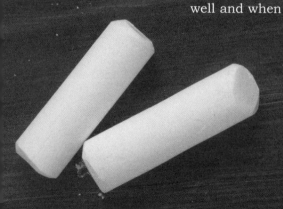

4   CLOSED QUESTIONING

One of the most bizarre delusions in teaching is the idea that open questions (ones with no single right answer) are inherently better than closed questions (ones with a single correct answer). They both have their place – there are things that open questions can do that closed ones can't. However, actually finding out if the class know the right answer to a particular question (often the recall of a particular fact) is crucial, and finding this out, quickly and effectively, is a vital skill. It is an important, maybe the most important, part of questioning.

5   SETTING TESTS (AND NOT JUST FOR ASSESSMENT)

It turns out that nothing aids memory of something better than being asked to recall it. This is called 'the testing effect' and can be easily found in the psychological literature (or on the internet if you prefer). It's far better than note taking. It's far better than highlighting in bright colours. Once you've realised the role memory plays in learning and thinking, then the obvious next step is to make use of this method of learning. Don't just set tests for assessment; set them as practice in remembering. You may also find that with some classes it has positive effects on motivation and behaviour too.

6   TELLING STUDENTS STUFF

I'm sure nobody has given up on this completely, but crazes for discovery learning, independent learning and group work often distract from this. Teachers often feel that they have to extract knowledge from students through a painful process of hints and guesses, getting students to look through a textbook or sending them to the nearest computer to research for themselves. Actually, there is good evidence, both from experience and from the research (particularly from the education programme known as Direct Instruction), that being told stuff by somebody who knows what they are talking about is a great way to learn. Obviously, it helps if you can make it interesting, or if you can't make it interesting you make it painless, but telling students the stuff they need to know (not just learning objectives, assessment criteria or how to do the latest zany activity) is a great way to get them to know it in the first place. You may have seen a graphic explaining that we remember different percentages of things depending on how we learned it, with being told having the smallest percentage. Don't worry, it's a pile of pants with no actual evidence behind it.

7   STAY AT THE FRONT

If you have a desk at the front of the room, use it. Some classes go off task when they feel they aren't being observed. Many students feel safer when they are being observed. So stay at the front where you can see them. When you want to see a student's work, or they want to ask you about something, make them come to you (one at a time, of course). Do not stop observing the class. Another advantage is that by spending more time sat down you save your energy for what really matters – the teaching.

8   LONG PIECES OF WORK IN THEIR BOOKS

One of the worst side-effects of the 'progress in 20 minutes' craze, not to mention the three-part lesson fad which preceded it, is that students often fail to spend a long time practising anything. Despite all the talk of learning 'skills', the most important part of learning a skill (i.e. practice) was often neglected. There are advantages to breaking up a task or revisiting it over time, but there are also advantages to spending a long time practising just one thing. It's OK if children do the same thing for one lesson, or even several lessons, if the aim is mastery. If we want our students to truly master what they are doing, and if we want them to be able to build securely on what they've done before, then they will need to practise not just until they get something right, but until they never get it wrong. This has long been accepted for playing a sport or learning a musical instrument, and it should apply equally to written work.

9   PUNISHING KIDS

If you think that an education is valuable, then stopping others from learning, except in the rare instance that this is a symptom of a medical disorder, is not simply a cry for help. It is not a justifiable reaction to not being ceaselessly entertained. It is the theft of something precious. It is morally wrong. It is deserving of punishment. Almost any child will tell you that doing bad things means you deserve something bad to happen to you. Only adults, and usually just a small minority of middle-class adults, ever lose sight of this.

Most schools recognise that good deeds need rewarding; this is just the same principle. So, let's be clear: disrupting lessons deserves a punishment. Not persuasion. Not a bribe. Not support with building a relationship with the teacher. It deserves something unpleasant to happen to the student who did it, and an apology to be given to those who lost out. Also, in schools where teachers are supported with discipline, it's a good behaviour management strategy, at least if your aim is for kids to learn. It works (not perfectly, but then nothing does), but, more importantly, it's just. Do it more.

10   LET KIDS BE DOWN

This is probably the most controversial thing I ever say, although ironically it's one of the things which has most scientific evidence behind it, far more than I could even begin to list here. We learn well when we are down. I don't mean traumatised. I don't mean living in a state of fear. I don't mean confined to bed with clinical depression (although evolutionary psychologists have claimed that depression may have evolved because it has, at times in our evolution, enabled us to learn more effectively). But the natural state of mind for deep analytical thought, or effective recall of knowledge, is not one of happiness. The natural expression for deep thought is pretty much a frown. We shouldn't make kids miserable or ignore real psychological problems, but it is a myth that kids learn best when they are happy. Also, if you are a grumpy teenager there are few things more embarrassing than an adult, particularly one who isn't close to you, trying to cheer you up. Let kids frown in your classroom – it may just help them think.

The sense of achievement and
success after a production
cannot be replicated

PERFORMING ARTS

LISA FERNANDEZ ADAMS @LISAFERNANDEZ78

1 Collaborative process. Putting on a musical is a big task. The production relies not only on the performers but on technicians, colleagues, parents, public, friends and family. The sense of achievement and success after a production cannot be replicated. Use each other's skills and expertise to good effect and always remember that a 'thank you' at the end of the process goes a long way!

2 Students appreciate personalised feedback to help develop their performance skills. Some successful ways of doing so include: written feedback relating to the criteria/mark scheme; using a Dictaphone to record comments in one-to-ones which students can then type out for evidence/target setting; annotating still images; and providing commentary of a performance over the top of the video footage.

3 Modelling skills and working methods. Show students you are not afraid to try new ideas and for them to go wrong, discard them and start again, or use ideas to springboard and create new ideas. Being creative in the rehearsal space should happen always – if not here then where?

4 Share your knowledge, successes and failures within your department – your colleagues are often your best teaching resource!

5 Explore career choices with your students and parents. Yes, it would be great to get on stage and be a performer, and we aim to give all students the best chance of achieving this goal. But you should also expel the common myth that 'there aren't many jobs in performing arts' which is so often expressed at open evenings. There is an abundance of jobs in the performing arts, so be explicit about them to show the rigour and opportunities that come hand in hand with this industry: actor, singer, dancer, presenter (radio, television), entertainer (singer, children's, cabaret), theatrical agent, choreographer, arts administrator, stage manager, lighting designer/technician, costume designer/technician, wardrobe assistant, hair and make-up artist, set designer/builder, prop maker, teacher (primary, secondary, sixth form, further, higher, private sector), sound engineer, marketing and events management, photographer, journalist, scriptwriter, community

education worker, therapist (drama, dance), music producer, director, etc.

6 If you don't ask ... In this industry, it is so often about who you know, so do not be afraid to ask a cast to do a Q&A with your students at the end of a performance, if you can work with a professional performer, if directors of drama schools will come along to see your students perform in their end-of-year show and so on. I have asked for all of the above, and all have said yes and it has often subsequently led to long-standing arrangements.

7 Expose your students to a range of styles, performance opportunities, working relationships, practitioners and genres within the performing arts to give them a breadth of knowledge. For musical theatre, for example, encourage your students to study jazz dance, contemporary dance, ballet, look at scripted work, monologues, devised work, physical theatre and realism, singing as a soloist and as a group. Students should also understand the context of performance work and analyse the social, historical and political context of performance. Look at budgets for putting on a show and allow students to design sets, lighting and costumes, as well as becoming actively involved in marketing.

8 Working with professionals can help not only to reaffirm your own knowledge and skills that you are teaching to your students, but also gives them a real vocational insight. Working with performers, directors, singing coaches, practitioners and technicians can be invaluable and extremely inspiring. And it can challenge your students even more since they are often keen to impress new faces! All of the work taught can then be used to feed into your own teaching, assessments and future planning.

9 Rehearse, rehearse, rehearse. Stress the importance of this to your students. They simply will not progress if they do not rehearse. I have used a reward chart with my students where they mark themselves after each lesson on a student chart and I mark my own teacher chart. When it comes to allocating a grade for the rehearsal and creative process, this can be an extremely useful and self-reflective tool for the students, as well as providing an accurate summary.

Standards in this industry need to be exemplary if students are to succeed, so set these same high standards in your own teaching space. Have high expectations but be fair and judge progression according to each individual.

> They simply will not progress if they do not rehearse

10 Expect and train your students to be a courteous and attentive audience for their peers, to listen to each other and respect each other's ideas, to contribute to the group and to work hard in every lesson. Every student should aim to progress each and every lesson, and a constructive working environment is key to this.

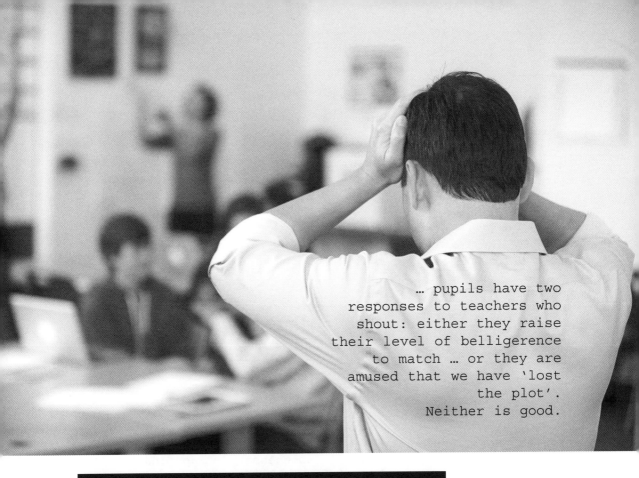

... pupils have two responses to teachers who shout: either they raise their level of belligerence to match ... or they are amused that we have 'lost the plot'. Neither is good.

BEHAVIOUR

@CAZZYPOT

1 DON'T SPEAK UNTIL THE WHOLE CLASS IS LISTENING

Wait as long as you need to. If pupils start talking while you're talking, stop and wait. Don't ever raise the volume or tone of your voice to try to talk over pupils. Also try not to shout. In my experience, the pupils have two responses to teachers who shout: either they raise their level of belligerence to match, which makes the situation worse, or they are

amused that we have 'lost the plot'. Neither is good. If you feel like shouting, try to train yourself to speak very quietly, or say nothing at all!

2 PARENT POWER

Not all parents are supportive, I know, but many are. Let the pupils know that you are prepared to ring home and discuss their conduct. Make sure you let the pupil(s) know this in advance, then do it. This also applies to good news. If something exceptional has been produced, tell the parents!

3   HAVE A SEATING PLAN

Don't ever allow groups of friends or like-minded individuals to sit together to the detriment of their education. Sometimes pupils won't like this, but lessons aren't meant to be an extension of their social time. Put the desks in rows if you want to. This can be useful if you are still trying to assert your authority over a certain group. I know it's unfashionable, but sometimes it can really help pupils to focus.

If you say you're going to do something, you must do it.

4   DON'T EVER MAKE A THREAT UNLESS YOU'RE FULLY PREPARED TO CARRY OUT

I learned this very early on in my career. If you say you're going to do something, you must do it.
(NB: This also applies to nice promises!)

5   GET PUPILS TO HAND IN BANNED STUFF OR KEEP IT AWAY

My working environment is a pupil referral unit (PRU), so the pupils don't get as far as the classroom if they don't hand in their fags and phones. I know this is almost impossible to enforce in a mainstream secondary, but don't ever turn a blind eye to kids who are fiddling with stuff. Give pupils a chance to put it away, then take it off them if they won't stop. Not just phones: take away any unnecessary paraphernalia.

6   DETENTIONS

Again, I know it's not always easy to enforce this but we must. If a child is given a detention, try everything in your power to make sure they attend. A supportive SLT can make all the difference with this one. If a pupil misses a detention, make a note and rebook it. If you let it slide, you lose credibility. Pupils hate missing out on their social time. Detentions can be a far more powerful weapon than we realise.

7   TIMED SANCTIONS

Closely linked to the above, but possibly more effective in a primary or PRU setting, try to take the same amount of time off the pupils as they have wasted of yours. For example, if a pupil takes 15 minutes to remove their coat and begin work, that's how long they owe you. Sometimes you may only need to see them for two minutes. Pupils will often perceive this as being more fair than, say, a 30-minute fixed detention.

8   BE HUMAN AND BE FAIR

Pupils have a highly developed sense of what is fair and what is unfair. Always try to be consistent. Be respectful of them, as you expect them to be respectful of you. If you're in the wrong or make a mistake, apologise. Show some humility, humour and self-deprecation, if appropriate. If you don't know the answer to a question, say so. All of these factors go a long way towards helping build solid pupil-teacher relationships. Don't underestimate the role of this in good behaviour management.

> There is an almost indisputably close link between pupils being proud of the work they do and the good behaviour that usually follows.

9   HAVE HIGH EXPECTATIONS

This goes for both work and behaviour. Encourage pupils to have pride in what they achieve. This includes handwriting and presentation. Praise them when they produce good work to show you notice. Make them start again if you know they can do better. There is an almost indisputably close link between pupils being proud of the work they do and the good behaviour that usually follows.

10   YOU CAN'T WIN THEM ALL

There will always be some pupils who you can't get through to. Try not to let this affect your confidence. Hopefully the school structures, behaviour policy and SLT are strong and effective enough for you to be able to remove such pupils. The majority should never have their education disrupted because of the conduct of a minority or an individual. If you're not winning, get them out.

1. **GET TO KNOW THE PEOPLE YOU ARE TEACHING**. Ask other members of staff about them. It is easy to forget that you are teaching a class of individuals. The quiet, unresponsive or challenging child might be hungry, scared or unable to trust. To teach them effectively you need to earn their trust.

2. **TREAT YOUR PUPILS WITH RESPECT AT ALL TIMES**. You will be respected in return.

3. **ASK YOUR PUPILS FOR FEEDBACK ON HOW YOU HELP THEM TO LEARN**. Listen to them and teach accordingly.

4. **KNOW YOUR PUPILS' CAPABILITIES AND UNDERSTANDING AND TEACH ACCORDINGLY**. Don't fit your pupils to your lessons. Adapt the learning to fit them.

5. **DON'T TALK TOO MUCH**. Let them get on with it!

6. **AFL IS WHAT YOU SHOULD BE DOING ALL THE TIME**. Every question, every conversation, tells you something about their learning. Use this in conjunction with marking to plan their next steps.

7   **MARKING MATTERS**. Feedback matters. If no one is going to look at their work, why should they bother? Feedback is the single most effective tool in enabling pupils to make good progress. It is also a great way to develop dialogues with individuals where you can provide further challenge and support. Remember what it felt like to get an unmarked book back when you were a child.

8   **BAN RUBBERS**. The fear of making a mistake can seriously inhibit learning for some people. Create a safe learning environment where mistakes are seen as learning opportunities. A crossed out mistake also shows you how that child is thinking.

9   **ENJOY YOUR DAY AND FEEL EXCITED ABOUT THE LEARNING JOURNEY AHEAD**. You create the climate in your classroom!

10 **LISTEN TO THE POSITIVE PEOPLE IN THE STAFFROOM AND IGNORE THE NEGATIVE ONES**.

11 (Cheating a bit, but it's important!) **ALWAYS HAVE HIGH EXPECTATIONS**. Your pupils will rise to them. Don't be a limiting force. Give them opportunities to surprise and delight you.

1 As soon as humanly possible, stop using your school's lesson planning pro forma. There are thousands of useful templates with which you can ensure your lesson contains all the required elements, but the one your school provides will almost certainly add an unnecessary layer of bureaucracy to an already demanding task. The best bet is probably to produce your own, tailored to your needs.

2 Ask to be observed. You've just finished your PGCE – you're used to people watching you teach – so, while the pressure is less intense, ensure you get as much feedback as possible from peers, mentors, other teachers or anyone else who might offer constructive advice. If you're feeling masochistic, film yourself.

3 Chances are you have your own classroom now – so make it yours. Ensure wall space is used effectively, whether that's by showing pupils' work, creating displays which will be used in lessons or by any other means. Anything in your room that isn't being used is a waste of space, so utilise your walls and whiteboards effectively – differentiation and extension tasks are so much easier to manage when you have an interactive classroom.

4 Front-load your teaching. Do your 'teaching' of knowledge and skills at the start of the week, then let your pupils work on developing these in the latter part. It relieves the planning burden, allowing you to focus on feedback as pupils put your teaching into practice. It's a much more energy-efficient way of working – for everyone.

5 Beg. Borrow. Steal. I have very few original ideas in my teaching, but I'm often complimented on my innovative approaches. I simply nod sagely, without admitting that I largely borrow from others – whether that's taking an existing scheme of work and adapting it to my purposes, ripping off a chapter from a book, using someone else's lesson plan or just asking for help. Twitter is absolutely invaluable for this, but your school ought to have a library with useful books by educators – and you work in a building full of people who can help: your colleagues.

6 Learn your school's behaviour policy inside out, upside down and back to front. The pupils know every loophole and will be merciless in taking advantage of gaps in your knowledge.

7 You're new, so you need to forge some kind of reputation. The best way is simply to get involved in things outside of your classroom: participate in sports day, take part in extra-curricular activities, do a break duty, go on school trips. Pupils and other teachers need to know who you are, and this is a quick and painless way of introducing yourself. You know those teachers who reveal nothing of themselves? Don't do that.

8 You're a person, so your pupils will appreciate knowing a little bit about you. Talk about sporting fixtures, bring music you like into your lessons, use personal anecdotes to illustrate the points you make. And find out about them. You don't have to be mates, but you do have to be human.

9 Look after your voice and body. Teaching is physically draining – you can't afford to skip the gym, eat badly, survive on coffee and/ or cigarettes.

10 Establish a routine. The first thing I do in the morning is select an album to listen to and drink a coffee. When the final bell goes I spend ten minutes catching up with the news. These little moments are vital. Your time is not your own as a teacher – you have to make time for yourself.

FOR NQTS

ROB WARD @PGCENG

You know those teachers who
reveal nothing of themselves?
Don't do that.

COLLABO[RATIVE]
WORKING

1 Pair up with other departments to collaboratively plan for next half term. Find out what skills/knowledge will be taught and make links that will allow pupils to apply new concepts to various situations. For example, art and maths could pair up to create a scheme on geometry and measures.

2 Reading, writing and communication are useful in every lesson. Create cross-curricular learning tools that pupils are explicitly taught how to use in English lessons, while other subjects ask pupils to use the tools to support them in tasks. Use CPD time to allow staff to practise using them. For more information see: http://thelearninggeek.com/2013/09/gap-splitt/.

ATIVE

LISA JANE ASHES @LISAJANEASHES

3 Don't be afraid to mash up subjects. Chris Curtis shows how fun and useful this can be here: http://learningfrommymistakesenglish.blogspot.co.uk/2013/08/mashing-up-literacy.html?m=1/.

4 Don't stay in your 'subject' comfort zone! Find out what your pupils are learning around the school and keep your eyes open for potential links. Sharing subject topics or overviews on a central VLE is a great way to keep up-to-date on what's happening out there.

5 Setting up teaching and learning communities, made up of teachers from as many subjects as possible, is a great way to sustain collaboration. Build in regular meeting times so that the communities can have mini TeachMeets and share best practice. Well planned, internal mini TeachMeets can be excellent CPD!

As part of your school's CPD programme, subjects could take turns in leading a best practice session for the whole school, demonstrating how they have put whole-school initiatives into practice. For example, if your school is beginning to use literacy mats, subjects that have been successful in integrating them into their lessons could share their success and provide top tips from their classrooms.

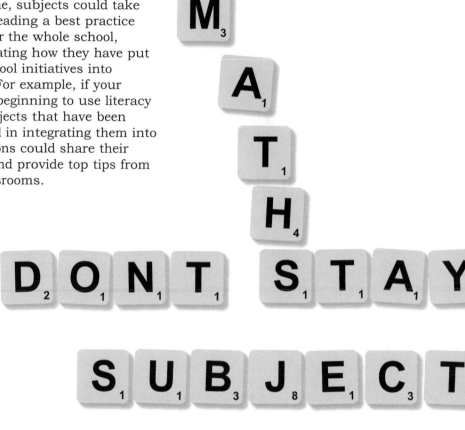

Mathematics is not a crime! There's maths in everything! Find out what pupils are being taught in maths next half term and look out for ways to help pupils practically apply their learning. If you're an English teacher and you really can't find an opportunity (I promise they exist), you can support pupils' mathematical growth by avoiding any negativity about the subject. Collaborate with maths to avoid another generation growing up seeing maths like Marmite.

8 Be brave! Collaborate with teachers across the curriculum on projects that may enhance your whole-school environment. You would need permission from the head teacher, but why not collaborate on a staff well-being project, learning outside the classroom, EAL provision, questioning projects, displays for learning ... The list goes on and on.

IN YOUR

ZONE

ENGLISH

9 Within subject teams, decide on an element of your subject that is difficult for pupils to grasp. Work as a team to plan a lesson with this as the focus. One person in the team teaches the lesson while the others observe the learning. Feed back as a team to dissect the learning and plan the next steps.

10 Remember, in a secondary school, you are one of many teachers your pupils are experiencing. Don't compete – collaborate for maximum results. As Peter Gloor of the MIT Center for Collective Intelligence says, 'Don't be a star, be a galaxy!'

MUSIC IN AND FOR EVERY LEARNING ENVIRONMENT

NINA JACKSON @MUSICMIND

Music is a universal language. It's quite simple really - it touches the hearts and minds of all human beings. Whether we understand why and how doesn't matter at this point - we just know that it can make a difference to our emotional state, from the way we think to the way we respond to situations, in life as well as learning.

Music is a powerful tool but it is still very much untapped and underused by many educationalists, mainly because they are unsure of its credibility as a tool to support learning, thinking and creativity and its overall benefits in the classroom and learning environment.

Trust me when I tell you that it *does*! I have done the research and the overwhelming conclusion is that using the right music for the right reasons and at the right time makes a difference in raising standards of attainment and achievement as well as personal well-being, behaviour, speech and language, in addition to supporting you as an educationalist.[1]

When choosing the right music for the classroom, it is essential that you consider many factors, including whether your choices fit the right criteria for using music as a learning tool. This includes beats per minute (BPM), frequencies, the use of lyrics and instrumentation, and whether it is acoustic or electronic. There is a science behind it, you know!

Here are six important questions to consider when it comes to making the right choices:

1. What type of emotional state do you want to create?

2. What is the right volume for the occasion?

3. Have you got music with the most appropriate instrumentation?

4. Do you need a piece featuring a soloist, jazz group or choir? Should it be electronic, orchestral or contain lyrics?

5. What is the age range of your learners? Bear in mind the generation gap – music that appeals to you might not always appeal to them.

6. Are your students working to the 'wrong' music? Do not let yourself or your learners fall into the trap of using any type of music which, in the long run, could have an adverse effect. You are searching for music that stimulates the mind and, when you find it, makes you enjoy the feeling as your neurons fire up and the first sweet strains of musically generated electrical energy flow through your cortex. Here are some suggestions you might want to use, but the secret to their correct use and application can be found in my book, *The Little Book of Music for the Classroom.*

---

1 For more on this see N. Jackson, *The Little Book of Music for the Classroom: Using Music to Improve Memory, Motivation, Learning and Creativity* (Carmarthen: Crown House Publishing, 2009), which is a consolidation of years of research on the effects of music on the brain.

MUSIC FOR LEARNING, MEMORY AND FOCUS:

This music is about getting the brain ready for learning – ready to recall information, to solve problems, to learn by rote, to develop study and revision skills and even to deduce theorems. I've found that focusing music can help learners and teachers with abstract reasoning, brainwork (e.g. analytical, creative or administrative thinking) and aspects of motivation. Music has the neural firepower to jazz up students' thought processes and reasoning skills. Listening to music can help them to encode information and improve the recall process. The right music at the right time can induce a mood of concentration, filter out any distractions and structure their thoughts for academic learning.

Music can also help learners to work smarter, not harder. The accelerated learning school, pioneered by Bulgarian psychologist Georgi Lozanov during the 1950s and 1960s, and later popularised in the United States by Sheila Ostrander and Lynn Shroeder, holds that learning in time to music of about 60 BPM helps to imprint material in the memory with less conscious effort. Learning to music is certainly an improvement on the usual grinding process of silent memorisation, so why shouldn't something that sounds good make the memory work better?

Certain kinds of music induce a receptive mood that generally enhances cognitive processing, that can serve as a mnemonic memory aid to help encode information in the mind and that supports initial learning, recall and transference into working memory.

Music primes the mind for learning, whether we are deducing mathematical theorems, drawing conclusions from experiments, playing chess or being challenged by abstract thinking. By using music correctly, you will be able to stimulate aspects of the learners' left brains in order to promote logical and analytical thinking, as well as stimulating right-brain thinking to help them grasp the big picture and think in a non-verbal and more creative way. Music also helps when they are studying for a test or examination or when they need to recall knowledge, information, shapes or pictures. Here are a couple of suggestions:

Liquid – 'Sweet Harmony' (original mix)

Mozart – Divertimento No. 11 in D major

Adolphe Adam – *Valse* from *Giselle*

MUSIC FOR RELAXATION AND CALM:

The ancient Greeks used music to calm the behaviour of belligerent drunks and as a 'medicine' for those who displayed unacceptable behaviour. In more recent times, Tyne and Wear Metro, drawing on a study in Canada in 2005, began playing classical music through speakers to disperse gangs of youngsters at Tynemouth, Whitley Bay and Cullercoats stations. Meanwhile, the London Underground has also flirted with the idea and has been running a pilot project at Elm Park station on the District Line in East London, apparently with some success. Relaxing music can quiet the nerves and free the flow of pleasant dream-like thoughts. Studies from the United

States to Shanghai show that listening to music promotes interaction and a sense of communal well-being, and that individuals direct their thoughts in a more focused way when music is playing in the background.

Music makes people more likely to say what they feel and it has been shown to induce significant improvements in relaxation, better moods and happier thoughts, even among learners with emotional and behavioural difficulties. Relaxing music can break down barriers and create shared social space through sound waves. It can also help to control social situations, keeping everyone feeling friendly and satisfied.

We live in a hectic and chaotic society which often seems overwhelming, given the amount of work and the number of daily jobs we are expected to carry out. Music can be used as a counterbalancing, inward-directed experience. In a learning environment, it will pull your pupils into their own sonic space, filtering out the noises and distractions that inevitably cause chaos at times. Using calming music will free the learners' consciousness from external concerns and help them to relax at a deep, inner level; it will support learning and emotional responses to tasks and activities in the classroom for yourself and your learners; it will get the learners ready for your lesson and improve behaviour; and it will set free the creativity of all learners and develop their creative thinking skills. Here are some music tracks you might want to consider using:

Ennio Morricone – 'Gabriel's Oboe' from *The Mission* soundtrack

Libera – 'Sanctus'

Hans Zimmer – 'Now We Are Free' from *Gladiator* soundtrack

MUSIC TO MOTIVATE, STIMULATE AND ENERGISE:

Music is audio fuel for action! When the sound of stimulating music hits the air and the inner ear, the cochlea converts it into electrical energy, sending it to the brain. In short, the right kind of music electrifies the body. Music that motivates, stimulates and energises can also produce beta waves in the brain – electrical patterns of around 13–30 cycles per second that help us with external events, to make quick decisions and to solve immediate problems. It may be a basic craving to be more awake in body and mind that makes people prefer music that moves at a faster speed and with higher pitches and brighter sounds. Stimulating music supports learners and teachers in becoming more motivated in their work and energised to learn and study.

As well as using music to aid learning, it is also a great way to make you and your students feel good about themselves. Lyrics can be just as powerful as purely instrumental sounds, and I recommend pieces that you can use to motivate, stimulate and energise learners, both in and out of the classroom. It's all about getting the mind, brain and body moving, not just in a motivational sense but in a physical sense too.

Energise your learners and get their bodies and minds working with up-beat, thrilling music. Too often in education we forget to celebrate what we have done well. We are always seeking the next thing rather than acknowledging what we have already achieved. So, don't just sit there. Think about what your students have done today that they should be proud of and should make them feel good about themselves. There is so much suitable music you can access for this, but make sure they are pieces with a tempo of between 100–165 BPM. Here are some suggested tracks:

Eddie Cochran – 'C'mon Everybody'

Van Halen (or Girls Aloud) – 'Jump'

Sounds of Blackness – 'You Can Make It If You Try'

A LITTLE WORD OF CAUTION:

Make sure when you are downloading any music that you have permission to do so. Many of us would rather pay a few pence for authentic recordings than cause waves with illegal downloads. You are the person who has to take responsibility for what you choose to access and download from the internet. If it is freely available, then you are able to use it in your work. However, be careful with some sites which may have made slight alterations to original recordings because they don't have copyright permission from the original artist. All schools should have a licence to play musical recordings for educational purposes. If you are unsure, then ask your head teacher or local authority.

As teachers, we can now use ICT to support and help us in every way, and using music well will make your teaching and the learning in your classroom truly spectacular. So, seek and ye shall find music for free – if you want it badly enough. Good luck with your treasure hunt!

Remember: the right type of music for the right type of reasons. You may not find the perfect music every time, but experience and application is the key.

TEACHING WITH LOVE

DEBRA KIDD @DEBRAKIDD

1. Smile like you mean it. Children's mirror neurones are highly alert to your mood and they'll mirror it back. Show them you like them and you'll see it reflected.

2. Remember that the harder they are to love, the more they need it. According to Gary Chapman and Ross Campbell, every child has an 'emotional tank' that they need topping up with love.[1] Children who run on empty can't love back; they are angry and confrontational. You can't top up their tank with conditional love – 'I'll like you if … ' It needs to be unconditional, so that they know that you like them whatever. Getting them to do what you need should never be connected with your approval of them as a person.

---

1 G. Chapman and R. Campbell, *The Five Love Languages of Children* (Chicago, IL: Northfield, 1997).

3. Have a strategy for 'packing up troubles' so that children are safe in your room. Over the years I have:

- Kept a suitcase by the door so that children could write down a worry and pack it away.
- Made a giant's earpiece out of a funnel and rubber piping so that little children could whisper troubles to the giant.
- Made a listening garden where children could tell their troubles to plants.
- Created a bother bin for writing down problems, balling them up and throwing them away.

Sometimes children need to understand that you know they're troubled, but they can't tell you this directly. These techniques help them to temporarily park their worries, and the fact that you bothered to make them shows the children that you care and understand.

4. Show them you remember their likes and interests by incorporating bits of music you know they enjoy to accompany a PowerPoint presentation or by bringing in books, magazines and articles about things you know that they're interested in. Always say, 'I saw this and thought of you', so they know it is no coincidence and that they matter.

5. Model forgiveness. Never tell them *they* are bad – draw the line between their actions and themselves.

6. Be consistent with your boundaries. Children with chaotic home lives need order at school – it is a sign of love to set and maintain those boundaries.

7. Talk about the people you love and explain why you love them – help them to understand what healthy loving relationships are like.

8. Don't give faint or insincere praise. Save it for when it's real and genuine and then celebrate. Always praise the deed and not the person – this is consistent with tip number 5.

9. Let them know they can always do better – there is always somewhere to go. Loving children isn't about letting them off the hook.

10. Tell them they are more than just grades, and prove it by knowing them beyond their target level. One good way to get an insight into their minds, interests and likes is by doing the 'I Am' poem with them – it's amazing what comes out. Read the instructions to the children: they write the first two words and then add their own according to the instructions.

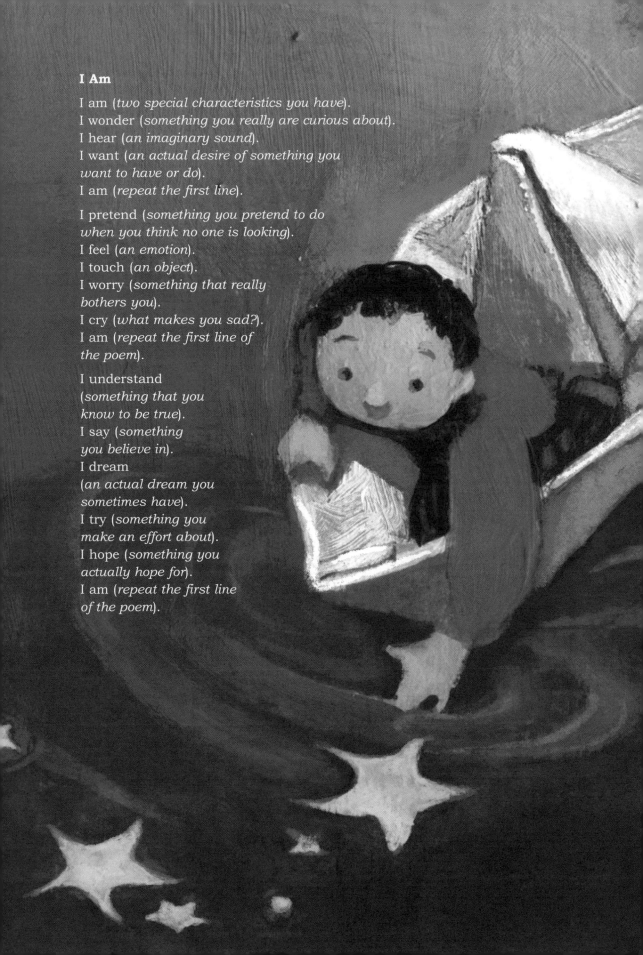

I Am

I am (*two special characteristics you have*).
I wonder (*something you really are curious about*).
I hear (*an imaginary sound*).
I want (*an actual desire of something you want to have or do*).
I am (*repeat the first line*).

I pretend (*something you pretend to do when you think no one is looking*).
I feel (*an emotion*).
I touch (*an object*).
I worry (*something that really bothers you*).
I cry (*what makes you sad?*).
I am (*repeat the first line of the poem*).

I understand (*something that you know to be true*).
I say (*something you believe in*).
I dream (*an actual dream you sometimes have*).
I try (*something you make an effort about*).
I hope (*something you actually hope for*).
I am (*repeat the first line of the poem*).

Educ

USING ICT
ACROSS THE
CURRICULUM

RACHEL JONES @RLJ1981

1 The first thing you need to know is that you shouldn't use ICT for the
   sake of using it. There are many lessons which would not be
enhanced by using ICT, so it is worth familiarising yourself with the SAMR
(Substitution Augmentation Modification Redefinition) and TPACK
(Technological Pedagogical Content Knowledge) models to give you the
confidence to know when to use technology to enhance learning and
when, as a professional, you can make a judgement that progress will be
achieved in the same way without it. You can find out more about these
frameworks at: http://createinnovateexplore.com/education-technology-return-
investment/.

2 If you are using an ICT suite, make sure you book it in advance, and for several sessions, to allow students to really develop their learning. If you find you don't need all the sessions you have booked, then sign the room back so someone else can use it. However, you don't need to be in an ICT suite to use ICT effectively in your lesson. My most successful use of ICT has been through making use of the devices that students bring into school with them. Many schools have dealt with the evolution in technology and smartphones by banning them, believing them to be a distraction to learning. In my experience, with the right ground rules in place, mobile devices can be used effectively in the classroom.

In order for this to happen you need to have developed mutual relationships of trust with your learners and have successful behaviour management strategies. You also need a suitable BYOD policy and have effective training in place to teach students about e-safety and leaving a digital footprint. In the same way that teaching literacy used to be the realm of the English teacher, issues around e-safety used to be the domain of the ICT teacher. No more. We are now all teachers of literacy, and it is every teacher's responsibility to keep children safe online and to help them understand the risks to their safety and reputation. For more information visit: http://www.swgfl.org.uk/Staying-Safe/.

3 Using ICT in your lessons is brilliant for helping students to extend their skill set that will be of use beyond school. For example,

why not try banning PowerPoint when learners give presentations and instead ask them to use websites such as PowToon, Haiku Deck or Prezi. In rethinking how they make presentations, learners are forced to rethink what they are presenting and how. It is a joy to watch some really well-thought-through presentations rather than watching students read text-heavy PowerPoint slides.

4 In terms of assessment for learning, a brilliant tool you can use is Nearpod. This is web based and allows you to upload an existing PDF or PowerPoint and then insert quizzes, polls, short answer questions and even a blank page that can be used for drawing a diagram or answer. Students can access this quiz on PCs or on mobile devices using an app, with which they then log-in to a room number. The teacher dictates the pace of the quiz and all the answers are made available throughout the course of the presentation. As the teacher can access all of the students' answers, this makes it an excellent tool for assessment. Plus, it's super easy to use.

5 Most devices allow students to make videos. You can use this in lessons to enable students to make videos that review learning content. However, you might also like to try creating a department or class YouTube channel to showcase and share work. Similarly, you can use the videos to flip your classroom, although this would tend to involve using video made by the teacher. Video and audio content is very powerful – for example, you can upload student-generated content onto

your school VLE for learners to use for revision. Students can then access these on their own devices, which will mean that they are becoming a community of self-supporting e-learners.

6 I am passionate about giving students a wider purpose in order to write to the best of their abilities. In terms of developing literacy skills, using ICT is extremely useful. Writing an essay no one will see, aside from the teacher, is basically a pointless task, unless it is part of formal assessment. If you allow students to write for a wider audience, literacy, engagement and enthusiasm will all increase. Blogging using sites such as AppShed to develop web-based apps and remixing programmes such as Hackasaurus provide opportunities to give student work real purpose, as well as demonstrate high expectations for the standards of work produced.

7 ICT can be used effectively to reward positive learner characteristics. You can use websites such as ClassDojo to reward mutually agreed behaviours, such as demonstrating resilience or recognising the purpose of redrafting. You can go one step further and reward learners with digital badges. There are numerous websites that allow you to do this, but my favourite is Credly, which enables the students to help design the badges, and thus they have real significance and meaning.

8 ICT can also be used to facilitate student-led learning. Try student-generated QR code treasure hunts or encouraging

students to reflect on their learning and progress by embedding media content in an Aurasma augmented reality trigger image. If you don't normally use ICT in lessons, please don't be put off by what might seem daunting difficulties. I am not an ICT teacher, and I have been able to use ideas like these to great effect to hand back the power in lessons to my learners.

9 Apps such as Sock Puppet and Puppet Pals are brilliant for developing higher order thinking skills. I have had huge success in progressing students' evaluative skills by asking them to create characters which then have to evaluate each other's point of view. Fun in itself, but also very meaningful learning that translates into exam success, as evaluative skills are highly rewarded in the exam mark schemes.

10 Try setting a digital alternative homework alongside more traditional tasks. Students can think creatively about using apps such as Vine to reflect on their learning, make a Pinterest board to reflect their research on a topic or make flash/quote cards using Quipio. The only limit here is your ability to curate their work (e.g. can they upload it onto the VLE?) and being confident about how you will give effective feedback.

Special thanks to @ICTEvangelist – Mark Anderson's blog is a treasure trove of ideas for using ICT in teaching.

USING RESEARCH IN SCHOOLS

CHRIS WAUGH @EDUTRONIC_NET

Teaching is an alchemy of intuition, experience, theory and enquiry. It requires from us the engagement of heart, body, mind and soul. As teachers we are part of the academic world, so there is a variety of ways that the first three, the subjective elements of our work, can be strengthened through active engagement with the fourth, through research. Here are some simple means, available to all teachers, that we can use to implement research as part of our everyday practice.

1 Teaching as enquiry. Firstly, due attention should be paid to the research practices inherent in our daily work. Classroom assessment in all its forms is a research practice of high value. Respecting this and ensuring that this assessment is always performed in the classroom setting with clear intent and a focus on ensuring its validity, whether it be diagnostic, formative or summative, is a research fundamental for all teachers. We spend our careers refining and improving this research capacity. A starting point for every teacher must surely be that we ensure we diagnose with precision, that our formative assessment is performed in such a way as to tangibly inform our ongoing work and that our summative assessment is clear, specific and effective in measuring our impact.

> Whenever we implement a new programme of learning or a new practice or approach in the classroom, we are engaging in research … we are providing ourselves with useful results upon which to measure our action

Getting these fundamentals right allows us to turn our classrooms into research environments, where we can explore and innovate and where we can be confident that we have in place the tools for measurement that allow us to come to meaningful conclusions. Whenever we implement a new programme of learning or a new practice or approach in the classroom, we are engaging in research, and if our assessment is up to scratch we are providing ourselves with useful results upon which to measure our action.

2 Make friends with researchers. Notwithstanding the existing classroom crucible, sometimes we have to seek fresh input and sometimes we want to know the impact of something before we are willing to take the risk of implementing it in our classrooms. The education world is bristling with university academics who are eager to work with teachers to engage in research. Building professional relationships with these people has the potential to bring to your practice the full weight of the research capacity of your local university and its resources. In doing this, not only will you gain detailed peer-reviewed and externally verified information about your classes and your practice, but also it is a brilliant way to learn about the research process on the job. This collaboration is almost always a win-win, and you'll earn the undying appreciation of your research friend in the process.

3 Read research and put it into action. There is a world of research knowledge already out there, just begging to be put into action in your classroom. Go to conferences, engage with your colleagues in the classroom and

online, join your subject association and read the articles in their research journal. As practitioners, it's not always incumbent upon us to perform research, but it's most certainly our professional role to keep ourselves informed and up to date with what research and theory tells us about our work. Why not set up a teaching book group with some colleagues and meet regularly to discuss what you've read?

4 Perform action research. Programmes such as Lesson Study are designed to be achievable in the day-to-day life of a teacher, and they encourage collaboration with teaching peers, mutual lesson observation and the discipline of devising valid research questions. The associated benefits of working together with a teaching peer and critically evaluating an aspect of your classroom work cannot be overstated. The professional conversations that arise as a result make the process worth it in its own right, even if the project doesn't succeed in making a tangible impact.

5 Use online tools. A good example of this is the Education Endowment Foundation's effect size calculator, which has been specifically developed to provide a summary of the aggregated findings of existing research in many areas of education.[1]

> Use research in every way you can, and always, always, keep that in proportion with what your heart tells you.

6 Don't forget how much you already know. Any time, say, an English teacher reads a novel or a classical history teacher goes on holiday to Greece, they are performing research in their own field of expertise that will benefit their classroom. As teachers we learn from everything around us; from a radio debate to the methods our running coach, yoga instructor or personal trainer use to keep us motivated, we're researching our work. We spent years learning about teaching before we started, many of us have been refining our work for decades and we're frequently evaluated in the work we do.

Teachers are constantly researching. Every time we come upon a useful artefact, we use our creativity and skill to put it into practice in our classroom.

Remember, education will always be an imprecise art. We work with human beings and this, in all our infinite complexity, will always defy objective classification. Use research in every way you can, and always, always, keep that in proportion with what your heart tells you.

1 Visit http://educationendowmentfoundation. org.uk/toolkit/.

Before we start, I would like to include an quick disclaimer. Myself and Amelia, who has helped me to write these tips, have a combined total of eight years of teaching behind us, so hopefully these suggestions are helpful – they are things that we have found to work during our relatively short teaching careers.

1   The subject is named 'design and technology' so try to keep abreast of the new technology out there now. Ask the students – they know what is currently hot and they will be more than happy to show you. In fact, this helps to grow a healthy two-way working environment.

2   Listen to older and wiser folk. More than likely, there will be a few people at your school who have seen it and done it all before. Technicians are great for this – they have often run their own departments in the past and, if you are willing to give them some time, a lot of useful knowledge is sure to come your way. For example, the most innovative lesson I've taught in the last six months was given to me by our technician, Jim. Thanks, Jim.

DESIGN AND TECHNOLOGY

DAVID BLOW @DTBLOW
AND AMELIA STONE @REVELLS7

3   Ever felt like you have repeated yourself 100 times teaching isometric or orthographic drawing? Sick of demonstrating how to thread a sewing machine? If you feel you are answering the same question over and over again, think about making a quick video that students can watch repeatedly, or better still get the students to make the videos themselves. Host them on your channel and be amazed at how many hits they receive.

213

4   Keep the workshops and design rooms open as much as possible. Students love to make things and experiment with materials and processes during their own time, and there is often a different feel to the environment outside of lessons. Practice does make perfect.

5   In the words of *The Hitchhiker's Guide to the Galaxy*, 'Don't panic'. Our subject can sometimes lead to keen and enthusiastic students who, when armed with chisels, can pose a significant health and safety risk. If you feel a practical session is getting out of hand, don't hesitate to stop everything, bring students around, calm down with a demo or discussion, make something up, anything to refocus the group before carrying on.

6   Know your students - differentiation by outcome is OK! All students will respond to a design brief differently and at different levels of complexity. Creativity varies from student to student, as does practical skill. By carefully judging the level of your class and the individuals within it, you can allow each student to produce projects that stretch their personal limits. If this is achieved, a truly mixed-ability group can progress through a task at a similar pace. Easier said than done!

7   Use e-portfolios. If you have the means, e-portfolios are great for adding interactivity and will allow students to play to their strengths. We have all spent hours verbally discussing a project with a student, only to discover later that they have included none of the content in their folder work, despite clearly understanding what they are doing. Utilising voiceover recordings, making videos and being able to communicate in ways not possible in a paper format opens lots of exciting doors.

Our subject can sometimes lead to keen and enthusiastic students who, when armed with chisels, can pose a significant health and safety risk.

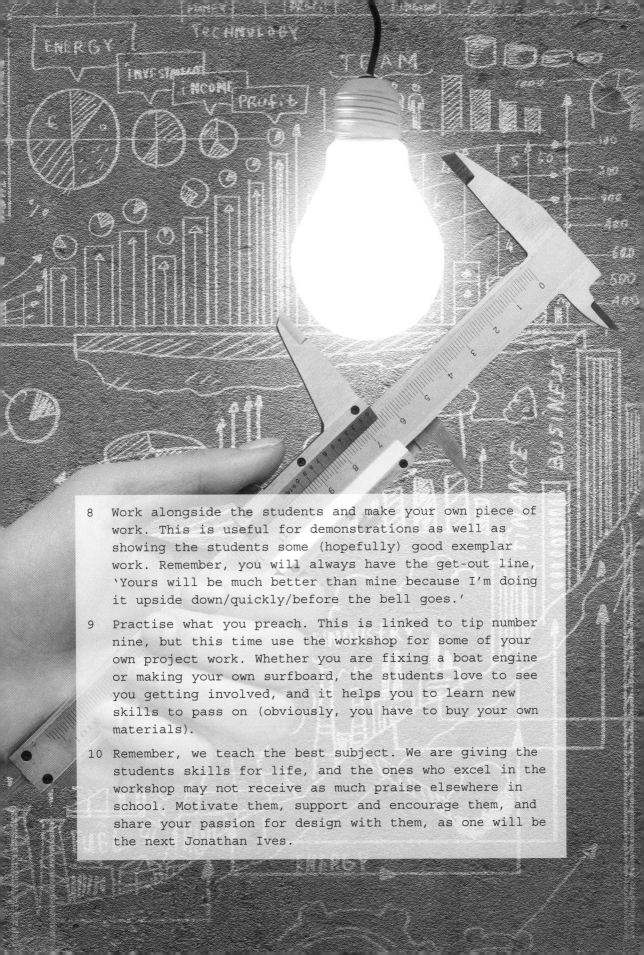

8   Work alongside the students and make your own piece of
    work. This is useful for demonstrations as well as
    showing the students some (hopefully) good exemplar
    work. Remember, you will always have the get-out line,
    'Yours will be much better than mine because I'm doing
    it upside down/quickly/before the bell goes.'

9   Practise what you preach. This is linked to tip number
    nine, but this time use the workshop for some of your
    own project work. Whether you are fixing a boat engine
    or making your own surfboard, the students love to see
    you getting involved, and it helps you to learn new
    skills to pass on (obviously, you have to buy your own
    materials).

10 Remember, we teach the best subject. We are giving the
    students skills for life, and the ones who excel in the
    workshop may not receive as much praise elsewhere in
    school. Motivate them, support and encourage them, and
    share your passion for design with them, as one will be
    the next Jonathan Ives.

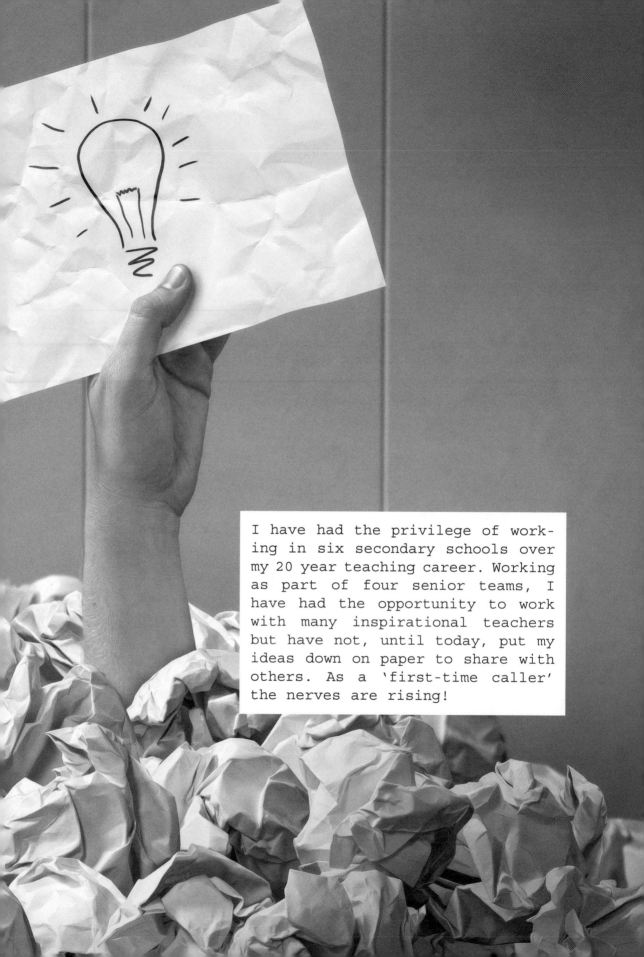

I have had the privilege of working in six secondary schools over
my 20 year teaching career. Working
as part of four senior teams, I
have had the opportunity to work
with many inspirational teachers
but have not, until today, put my
ideas down on paper to share with
others. As a 'first-time caller'
the nerves are rising!

SHARING RESPONSIBILITY IN SCHOOL

MARTYN REAH @MARTYNREAH

The list of tips below, which has become my way of working, has developed over time by observing how others work. I have been lucky to meet some very inspirational people in my six schools (Graham, Rick, Christine and Betty, to name but a few), but I have also met others who have taught me how not to do things. Whatever the circumstance and whatever the situation, the job, for me, is about continuing to learn and developing positive working relationships with all. Schools are schools despite the socio-economic background of the students and teachers, so hopefully you might find an idea to take back to your school to try out.

1 Encourage ideas. In my head, I am the same teacher as the one that started out in 1994. As school leaders, it is vital to remember the frustration of what it was like to teach 22 out of 25 lessons in a week and trying to get your voice heard. Developing formal and informal opportunities to discuss improvements with staff is a must. Teaching and learning breakfasts with croissants has worked well. Internal and external TeachMeets also fit the bill. If a teacher shares a way of improving how the school works, then it is my responsibility to support them to make it happen.

2 Go and visit. When I started teaching, I found it difficult to work to a timetable and to meet the demands of the job. I was stuck in a box (my classroom) and the interactions I had with more experienced staff involved removing difficult students or getting talked at during INSET days. I wasn't encouraged to talk about my problems. As a senior leader, I have the privilege of controlling my time and have the opportunity to get into classrooms to spend time with teachers and students. Hopefully in a non-threatening way! Leaders need to develop listening skills and the ability to react in non-defensive ways to feedback.

3 Make time. When working in some teams I have found it difficult to understand what is required of me. In order to gain some direction, I think it is important to be clear about what is expected. In many different ways I work hard to give time to staff as part of their working week. Meetings are the first things to get booked into the diary and I work hard to keep an open office door to encourage conversations.

4 Encourage collaboration, (5) Plan together and (6) Press the flesh. Starting my career in a small school in a small department was a challenge, and the history teaching I was asked to do, with very little support from others, nearly finished my career before it had started. As a leader, time spent with others focused on talking about teaching and delivering lessons can sometimes get lost in an annual CPD plan. Working in groups of three or four across departments on projects each individual has chosen (thanks Barbara and Christine) first developed my interest in joint planning and working as a team. This developed more through the excellent TEEP programme (http://www.teep. org.uk/) which provides a structure for this type of work. Watching and listening to teachers talk about this programme evokes an emotional response. They get evangelical about it. Not bad for whole school CPD (thanks Carly, Christine and Gary).

> I now encourage staff to take control of their own learning and decide how they want to develop and what they want to improve.

7 Twitter and (8) Keep learning. As a young teacher, I watched more experienced teachers and how they continued to learn. During school-based sessions, I watched some staff think about other things rather than the topic of the INSET/ meeting. Had they heard it all before?

I now encourage staff to take control of their own learning and decide how they want to develop and what they want to improve. Like the TEEP programme, the philosophy behind how Twitter works will stick with me for the remaining 25 years of my career. Supporting and watching others learn via Twitter has reshaped my understanding of professional learning which motivates, inspires and has impact!

9 Allow yourself to learn from those around you. Working as a head of year, my deputy head explained my job description to me, which involved 'advising' parents. This took me some time to understand as a 23 year old. How could *I* help parents with their children! It took me a while to grasp the key concepts of the job, but I had been lucky enough to start working in my first (very varied) well-led team. Colleagues helped me. External advisers helped me. My line manager helped me. But it still took time for me to get it. I still think that it takes some time to get used to the demands of the job and the stresses and strains, as well as what life throws at us. Not many teachers come into the job for the money. Most come to make a difference, as corny as that sounds. The more time we spend supporting the staff and understanding what they are interested in, the happier the school and the more the children will thrive. That's my opinion anyway.

10 Drink more water (thanks Patrick).

BUSINESS AND ENTERPRISE

Business and enterprise education is crucial to young people's employability and future economic well-being. It provides an opportunity for students to develop as individuals and become enterprising young people. Business enterprise education should be viewed not just as producing the entrepreneurs of the future but equipping students with the skills they will need in the future. Being enterprising can mean simply taking the initiative, having a positive attitude or seeing an opportunity. Enterprise skills include the following:

- Creativity
- Innovation
- Reliability
- Punctuality
- Positive attitude
- Team work
- Leadership
- Willingness to learn

- Seeing an opportunity
- Taking risks
- Initiative
- Communication
- Presentation skills
- Problem solving
- Ethics
- Drive to make things happen

These skills can be applied throughout the curriculum and can help students to achieve. I believe passionately in business and enterprise education and the opportunities it brings with it. I have seen students develop in confidence and motivation by taking part in enterprise activities, learning about business and developing their skills. Here are my top tips for business and enterprise:

STEPHEN LOGAN @STEPHEN_LOGAN

219

1 OPPORTUNITY

Business studies provides an opportunity to bring what is going on in the world into the classroom. Encourage students to be aware of current business and economic issues. Spend time discussing these and the impact they have on the economy in lessons. Choose topics and businesses that engage students.

2 SKILLS

Skills are as important as the curriculum content. This will probably open up a debate and is controversial, so I'd better explain it. What I mean by this is that students should be put in situations that develop their skills as well as their knowledge. This is part of lifelong learning and employability. At the start of every business course I have ever taught, I always explain this to students and constantly remind them of it with the types of activities and opportunities given.

3 VISITS

Visit as many businesses as possible. I have found that visits to employers, universities and conferences can be very powerful experiences for students. Students get so much from learning about the world of work from an employer. It enables them to experience and see business theory in practice. It's not just about the visit though – there is lots of potential learning in the prior research and subsequent reflection. Can business and education work together? Are these two worlds so different?

Another aspect is getting employers to co-deliver part of the curriculum. This enables students to delve deeper into businesses and find out first hand what they do. A key to this is finding the right people, who are engaging and can communicate with students on their level. Preparation, again, is essential for the students. It's not just about going on the visit – they should prepare questions and research the business in advance. We have some businesses that give support regularly and others who give it maybe once in a year.

4 SOCIAL MEDIA

Share, collaborate, design and discuss. Are you on Twitter? Are you on LinkedIn? Do you have a business studies school Twitter account? I have found these methods to be invaluable in engaging with local businesses to develop curriculum opportunities for students. Questions can be sent out and elicit a quick response. It provides another form of communication to enhance the curriculum.

5 ENGAGE

This is a key area for me. Are you a member of your local business networks? Do you attend business events? Some have membership costs to join, but it is really worth it from the benefits it can bring. Getting face to face with businesses provides a great opportunity for your own CPD as well as developing partnerships for visits and first-hand information. I rarely use textbooks when teaching business studies – the minute they are printed they are out of date.

6 INVOLVE

Ask students what they would like to study. Yes, I know there are specifications and timescales; however, there can be choice. In the seven years I have taught business studies, I have never taught the same business area twice. Students have chosen the sectors they wish to study.

7 COMFORT ZONES

This is about giving students opportunities to step outside their comfort zone. Essentially, it is about learning new skills. When students enter employment, they will need to develop skills such as presentation, teamwork, leadership, literacy, numeracy and communication. Although it's going to be difficult, and it's going to be a challenge, it's about being enterprising. If students step outside of their comfort zones then they are better placed to learn new skills and prepare for the challenges they will face in the ever-changing workplace. Take iOS developers or Zumba fitness instructors; these jobs didn't use to exist. Key to this is working in partnership with employers, colleges and training providers. By sharing skills with students that employers will expect, such as being enterprising and ethical decision making, we prepare them for employment.

8 UNLEASHING ASPIRATION

Find out why your students have chosen business studies. What are their career aspirations? Do they want to start their own company? There is a clear link between business and careers. Students can learn about businesses, career routes and also what employers they looking for. Our role as teachers is to unleash aspiration not only with a grade but with skills for the future.

9 ETHICS

This is a subject that continues to develop in the curriculum. Why am I including it in my top tips? The main reason is because it is topical and enables students to make informed decisions. In a global world, how do we instil in students the need to do things for the right reasons and not just for the profit line?

10 ENTERPRISE

I started this section of top tips with enterprise and I leave it as my final tip. I have explained and outlined this from a student perspective; however, how are you enterprising as a teacher? How do you create the opportunities and challenges to bring a great subject like business studies alive? You won't find the answer in a textbook! I hope I have given you a few tips, but you are the one who can make it happen.

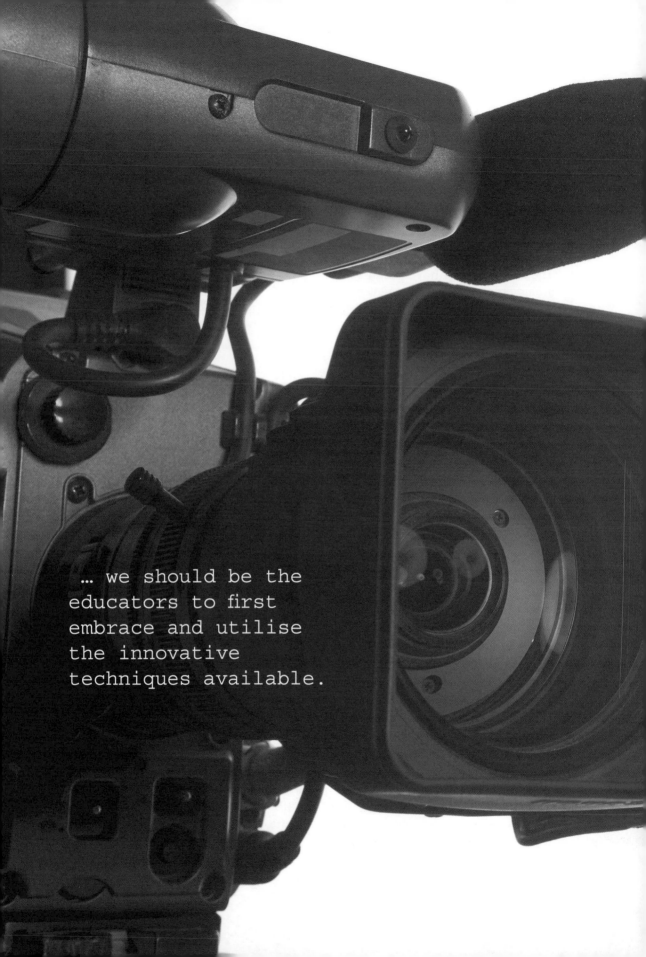

... we should be the educators to first embrace and utilise the innovative techniques available.

MEDIA STUDIES

SCOTT HAYDEN @BCOTMEDIA

As media teachers, I feel that we are in a privileged and unique position to be able to use creative and innovative educational tools and methods for a generation that is immersed in fresh and original modes of communication.

We can be the first to try new technologies and, because it falls within our subject specialism, we should be the educators to first embrace and utilise the innovative techniques available. It is the need to adapt and multi-task in this terrain that will become essential to helping our learners become the next generation of media producers that will inspire and shape future perspectives.

I love my job and believe that we should be pushing things forward in the use of educational technology to help our students. The following ten tips are some ideas that, in my experience, will help everybody.

1 VLOGS. Recording video feedback for your students allows you to provide more detail in less time than written feedback, while utilising a visual format your learners are engaged with all the time online (e.g. YouTube, Skype, Google+ Hangouts). By turning on your phone/tablet/web camera, you can record reflections and analyses of their work which can then be shared with them online.

The immediacy of your learners being addressed down the lens by you – calling them by name, using specific examples, referring to their work directly and speaking to them in a personal manner – will elicit similarly thoughtful reflections and improvements in their future work.

Vlogs are also incredibly useful ways for your students to respond to formative and summative assessment (e.g. debates, diary reflections, news reports) as well as providing opportunities to enhance their communication skills and demonstrate how they can articulate a response to a brief verbally rather than through endless written assessments.

2 PODCASTS. Feedback for your students work can also be recorded quickly and efficiently as a podcast. Students can listen to it from a device while looking over their work ('Now turn to page 10, paragraph 2. You have used the term post-modernism, but please add an example of this term ...) and pause it as and when they need to. The aim is to provide feedback that the learners will really pay attention to and that will take you less time to produce than another barely read set of annotations on a printed-off essay.

As with vlogs, your students can also record podcasts themselves on their devices, perhaps critically analysing media (e.g. use at least three media terms in a two minute vlog), discussing topical issues (e.g. courtroom/quiz show set-up) or reflecting on their experiences throughout a project (e.g. production diary, week 5).

The volume of evidence that the learners accrue throughout your lessons can be easily captured using the devices they are carrying and then uploaded to whatever space you are using to store work. Encouraging the students to take responsibility and ownership of their work goes even further to embedding the employability skills that will serve them well in their future careers (e.g. 'To submit your work, please upload to SoundCloud and link to your blog by 3 p.m.').

> The volume of evidence that the learners accrue throughout your lessons can be easily captured using the devices they are carrying and then uploaded to whatever space you are using to store work.

3 FACEBOOK. I know that many educators are reticent of using Facebook with students, but it is a standardised space that many students are using outside of class. Facebook can be used to share YouTube videos, Prezis and other information pertaining to that day's learning, while also allowing learners to interact with lecturers/peers outside of class. It can also be used to help the learners build a professional digital footprint and learn how to communicate in a mature and effective manner with one another in team projects (e.g. print screens which can be used as criteria evidence).

Students can curate and share content (e.g. memes, videos, articles, their own blogs/podcasts/vlogs, pictures) and can even create their own subgroups and 'Add me' to oversee their interactions/ideas generation, problem solving and organisation. The emphasis on autonomous learning is served by Facebook's inherent need for admin, clear communication and self-responsibility.

The students can connect their Facebook accounts to other social media. We use Tumblr for teamwork evidence, LinkedIn for career promotion, Twitter for our #bcotmedia daily debates, WordPress for journalistic work and Google+ for individual tasks. Facebook is the space they have grown up with, so it is where 80% of them gravitate back to for sharing ideas.

Students receive their video and podcast feedback from me directly into their inbox – I know they have received it and that it won't be lost. I have also started using the audio recorder function on the inbox Messenger, which is very useful. I also post job opportunities, work experience, university information, events, screenings and so on to help the students reach the next stage of their careers.

The learners have a safe, supportive, fun and encouraging space to share ideas, ask questions, get feedback and build their confidence and self-esteem at a time when they can be fragile and unsure. Student course reps can also hold group chats with other students to improve aspects of the course before feeding back to heads of department, thereby providing true learner voice and action.

> ... having [professionals] answer your students' questions on a set hashtag is a good way to take learning above and beyond the classroom

4 **TWITTER**. Hashtag debates to get each day started are simple and easy to curate. The theme of your lesson can be set up through a question to your students (something from that day's news works well), which comes with a hashtag you want them to tweet in on (e.g. Did Lena Dunham sell out her principles by appearing Photoshopped on Vogue? #bcotlena).

The tweets can then be displayed on your screen using Twitterfall or TweetBeam, and followed up on for directed and Socratic questioning, now they have already contributed to the discussion (getting over the nerves of talking first in class). The subsequent discussion can lead you in to your first objective.

It can also be of value to live-tweet during an event. My students and I followed up our lectures on representation with live tweeting during Ricky Gervais's *Derek*, which led to ethical discussion at 9 p.m. on a Thursday between 30 teenagers about the morality of media representation (e.g. Do you think Gervais is making fun of those with learning needs? #bcotderek).

In addition, connecting with other professionals and having them answer your students' questions on a set hashtag is a good way to take learning above and beyond the classroom, while also providing an experience of intellectual debate and enquiry for your group.

5 **TUMBLR**. The number of resources available to educators can be difficult to manage at times, so a set space for the learners to go to document their own work or access your resources is something that has helped me enormously throughout my career.

To manage my work, I have set up a handy cloud tag, bcotmedia.tumblr.com, as a space for me to post photos, videos, dictionary definitions, memes, reminders, help and tutorials for reference throughout the year. This is a revision aid for my learners and helps me to differentiate for the less and more able as they can go over materials from lectures and accompanying mixed media exemplars that further illustrate points. My lecture on psychoanalysis, for example, may have missed the mark but my GIFs, memes and videos about Freud may help to consolidate and make sense of the ideas gleaned from the lecture.

My students also have their own Tumblr blogs for different projects in order to keep their work separate, to organise it professionally and to store it in the cloud for easy access. Learners upload photos, videos and short text posts throughout projects to tell the story of their process and reflect at each key point on the journey towards the deadline.

The learners take pride in their blog and can have it marked via podcast or vlog at formative points throughout the project. This can then be linked to the student blogs as evidence of your marking and a reference point as to what they need to do next.

6 **GOOGLE DRIVE.** Your students can create text, spreadsheets, forms and presentation documents for projects that are saved in the 15GB storage space (and so cannot be lost). The teamwork in media studies lends itself particularly well to the collaborative nature of Google Drive's text documents. For example, your students could form groups of three and then simultaneously make notes from your lecture in one text document using different coloured text. The students will produce three times as much as they normally do and will soon be ready to refine the notes and create a podcast using them as a script for a critical thinking podcast discussion.

The storage space in Google Drive is also incredibly useful to back up the audio, video and text files that the learners will create throughout the year. As students tend to move between different classrooms and home to produce their final pieces, having the notes always centrally accessible from the cloud is a wonderful thing (e.g. 'I'm editing this right now on my phone').

7 **VINE.** Video is an invaluable and inventive way for learners to evidence their understanding of what they have learned – something that our subject actively encourages. As media students do not need to provide information through Word documents alone, they can use the ever-changing range of media platforms to articulate their

> My lecture on psychoanalysis, for example, may have missed the mark but my GIFs, memes and videos about Freud may help to consolidate and make sense of the ideas gleaned from the lecture.

understanding and knowledge in creative and imaginative ways.

Vine is an app that allows learners to film six second looping clips and then tweet them with appropriate tags. The chances that there are at least five smartphones in your class are high, so get them into groups to evidence their understanding of what you have taught them visually (e.g. Sell me the new iPhone in six seconds – #bcotad; use mise en scène to portray a positive representation of a female singer songwriter – #bcotrep; demonstrate Todorov's cultural theory in a six second narrative – #bcotstory).

> Industry professionals increasingly use the cloud to share and collaborate on projects, so students need to do the same.

The ability to be succinct and creative through the format is a neat and tidy way to gamify your objectives and check on their learning (e.g. Define the term 'ideology' in six seconds). You can get involved as well by recording yourself delivering a message to your learners, reminding them of key information or capturing a cross-section of the energy of your lesson to help promote your courses.

8 **INDUSTRY LINKS**. Local companies often want to be seen helping educational establishments. The positive press, mutual learning, potential work experience and apprenticeships for all parties concerned make it a great addition to the curriculum. Inviting in local media companies, connecting online or going directly to them in person will elevate the experience of the learners' work.

When my students know that Hello You Creatives, for example, will be looking at their blogs/portfolios, it crystallises their focus and purpose – they want to impress. The chance to work alongside advertising professionals and have their work seen beyond the classroom brings out the best from the students.

Sponsorship from industry raises the quality of the work, connects to the workplace and enhances staff professional development. It becomes about more than just a grade and starts to be a chance for students to prove themselves to observing eyes. The need to prepare young people for industry by teaching in combination with industry galvanises the learners. It has consequences. It will be seen.

9 **CLOUD STORAGE**. Industry professionals increasingly use the cloud to share and collaborate on projects, so students need to do the same. Our students tend to work with multiple assignments at any given time, so having an organised online space to save work that will never be lost can be a useful thing indeed.

Create a Dropbox account and insist that every learner create one from your shared link, which will then give you 500MB of extra storage per student account created. This will give you enough space to store your vlog/podcast feedback to share with your students as and when they need it.

Google Drive and SkyDrive are also great tools and come in handy when a team member is absent ('Have you checked your group cloud?').

10 COLLABORATION. Use social media to connect with other media teachers and start competitions with other institutions. Lecturer Peter Hearn has worked with his students to produce the feature film #Scrawl at Alton College in Hampshire. I have produced and directed music videos for @therunnersclub and @redtailsbanduk with media, make-up, photography and journalism students from Basingstoke College of Technology on set. After getting in touch via Twitter, Peter and I will be collaborating and moderating a 'Webisodes – Viral Campaign' project this year. Our respective students will create viral marketing and an eventual pilot, *Webisode*, for an original online series in a cross-college competition. Local media companies, Face TV and Pork Chop Pictures, will attend a screening and award the winners with work placements and a prize.

By tying every assignment to a third-party client who can contribute to the project remotely via Skype, come in for a guest lecture or award the best final pieces in the presence of the local press, the project comes alive in a way that the learners respond to directly – it becomes real.

The aim to raise the stakes and bring their work to as near professional levels as possible is essential for the students in order to truly prepare them for the next stage of their careers – something I wish I had had as a student.

I always want to collaborate with other media teachers, so please get in touch to start a project with my glorious #bcotmedia students.

I really hope some of these tips are of use to you and that I hear from some of you soon.

Remember who inspired
you to become a teacher

- you owe them.